The Python

Spirit

is sent to

STRANGLE
OUR SUCCESS

I0176614

APMI Publications
a division of Alan Pateman World Missions
P.O. Box 17,
55051 Barga (LU),
Tuscany, Italy

The
Python

Spirit
is sent to
STRANGLE
OUR SUCCESS

DR. ALAN PATEMAN

APOSTLES ARE DOOR OPENERS

BOOK TITLE:
The Python Spirit is sent to Strangle our Success

This edition published in 2025

Published by APMI Publications
A Division of Kingdom Dimension Books, Library No. **78**
P.O. Box 17,
55051 Barga (LU),
Italy

Email: publications@alanpatemanworldmissions.com
www.AlanPatemanWorldMissions.com

**APMI Publications and Kingdom Dimension Books are a division of
Alan Pateman World Missions**

Printed in the United States of America, Europe and Asia

Paperback ISBN: 978-0-9570654-8-2
eBook ISBN: 978-0-9570654-7-5

Acknowledgements:
Author/Design/Senior Editor/Publisher: Apostle Dr. Alan Pateman
Editing/Proofreading/Research: Dr. Jennifer Pateman
Computer Administration/Office Manager: Dr. Dorothea Struhlik
Cover Image Credit: www.PosterMyWall.com

*Where scriptures appear with special emphasis (**in bold,** italic or <u>underlined</u>) we have edited them ourselves in order to bring focused attention within the context of this subject being taught.*

We Occupy Until He Comes.
Luke 19:13

❖

Table of Contents

❖

Preface

In this book we step into the extraordinary story of Paul's apostolic journey through Philippi and how God used the apostolic ministry to change the course of history. This book is not about darkness or the demonic — it's about the power of the apostolic ministry to open spiritual doors and overcome profound opposition.

Acts chapter sixteen marks a pivotal moment in church history. When Paul set his sights on Asia, the Holy Spirit redirected him to Macedonia, Europe's spiritual gateway. This divine strategy echoed the Spirit's brooding over creation in Genesis, now preparing Europe for the arrival of the gospel. Yet, this historic mission faced fierce resistance — a Python spirit, manifesting through a seemingly harmless slave girl, sought to constrict the advance of God's kingdom.

This book explores how the Python spirit operates; just as a natural python suffocates its prey, this spiritual force seeks to quench the life and authority of apostolic ministries — through financial restriction, spiritual exhaustion, and cultural resistance. But Paul, a pioneer and one of God's "big guns," demonstrates how the apostolic ministry carries unique authority to confront these forces, open doors to new territories, and usher in revival.

With insights into the influence of the Oracle of Delphi and the cultural grip of divination in ancient Greece, The Python Spirit reveals the depth of spiritual battle that sought to block the gospel from touching down in Europe. Yet, through obedience, prayer, and divine power, Paul and his companions broke through, laying a foundation that transformed the world.

Whether you're called to apostolic ministry, fascinated by spiritual warfare, or eager to see how God's strategy unfolds in history, The Python Spirit will challenge, inspire, encourage you as it offers a profound look at how spiritual pioneers overcome the enemy and release God's purpose.

So, are you ready to see how apostles change history? Are you ready to break free from the constraints and see God's mission fulfilled? And are you ready to discern the times, open doors for the gospel, and stand in your God-given authority? Then step into the journey and be reminded that God is using the apostolic to OPEN NEW DOORS today. Be available, and be part of the divine mission and be used by God today.

❖

Foreword

This book titled, "The Python Spirit is sent to Strangle our Success" authored by Apostle Dr Alan Pateman, delves into the spiritual conflicts that hinder the propagation of the gospel. It underscores the necessity of apostolic authority, to surmount these impediments, drawing parallels to the efforts of Paul and his team advancing the gospel in Macedonia - Europe.

The text advocates for all Christians to partake in spiritual warfare to reach success, referencing Acts 16:16. "Now it happened, as we went to prayer, that a certain slave girl possessed with a spirit of divination met us, who brought her masters much profit by fortune-telling."

Furthermore, it posits that the book will equip readers with the requisite tools to navigate these challenges effectively. The author explains how the apostolic authority is instrumental in overcoming obstacles in the propagation of the gospel. It embodies the spiritual power and leadership that apostles have, enabling them to confront and surmount challenges that impede the spread of the gospel.

He said, this is rooted in the divine mandate given to apostles, empowering them to perform miracles, provide guidance, and offer protection against adversaries. By exercising apostolic authority, apostles can effectively dismantle barriers, inspire believers, and foster a conducive environment for the gospel to flourish. This concept is exemplified by the effort of Paul in advancing the gospel in Europe, as highlighted in the book, "The Python Spirit is sent to Strangle our Success."

I encourage all believers to have a copy of this material it will systematically empower and position you strategically to engage in proper warfare to live in victory.

Apostle Dr. Benjamin Ayim Asare,
Followers of Christ International Church, Novara–Italy
author of *The Anointing is the Assignment,* and
Discover Your Ministry in the Local Church

❖

Acknowledgement

*Just want to thank my wife Jennifer
for her love and support while writing this book,
and for her writing skills, research,
insights and inspiration.*

❖

Introduction

APOSTOLIC GATEKEEPERS

It has been my desire for many years, to fully understand the true nature of the apostolic ministry and it's God given authority within the SPIRITUAL GATES (places of spiritual authority). This book is a continuation of that desire, to help unravel the mystery of the apostolic ministry and its continuing role in the church and in the nations today.

Of course the main role of every apostolic ministry, is to reflect THE APOSTLE, Jesus Christ. Today, working *with* Him, there is still an important ongoing role that they must play, especially in this end time scenario. Their voices must be heard in the territorial gates of cities, regions, countries and nations.

And they went out and preached everywhere, while **the Lord was working with them** and confirming the word by the signs that followed.

Mark 16:20 AMP

The GATES are where those in authority gather. Those who get to decide what goes on in those territories. And there are gate-keepers. Those who stand for righteousness or darkness. Those with legitimate or illegitimate (lawless) spiritual authority.

IT IS GOD'S INTENT NOW THAT:

...through the church, the manifold wisdom of God should be made known to the rulers and authorities in the heavenly realms.

Ephesians 3:10 NIV

...to unveil before every throne and rank of angelic orders in the heavenly realm God's full and diverse wisdom revealed **through the church.** TPT

So, the question is this, who in the church reveals the wisdom of God to these authorities in heavenly places? Is this a joint effort or is this specifically for God's elite special forces? Answer: All of the above.

To help break this down, now let's go more deeply into the role of the apostles and reveal them in their sharpest focus.

Think Nehemiah, whom the bible describes as someone moved by God to *rebuild* the broken walls of Jerusalem, in doing so he also dealt with many gates, each with a specific purpose (read Nehemiah chapters 1-6).

Likewise, there are many gateways into our lives. We must be good gate-keepers (both individually and corporately), and learn to work *together* as the body of Christ, especially with those God has chosen to be gatekeepers on a bigger scale.

Scripture reveals that as believers, we are many members of one divine body, with legitimate authority on this earth, to continue the work of our Lord. **"The Son of God appeared for this purpose, to destroy the works of the devil"** (1 John 3:8 AMP).

We are a powerful body, especially when we work together (Psalm 133:1) and not disjointed (Mark 3:24-25). As we remain in Christ, being members of His body, the GATES of hell cannot prevail against us (Matthew 16:18).

CONNECTING FOR EXCELLENCE (DIVINE NETWORKING):

When it comes to authority structures, generally speaking gates are not places of relaxation. They are places of much spiritual activity, where access is granted or denied and where important decisions are made, for the entire region or place.

Gates were the place to get things done and to meet others in positions of influence or authority. A public meeting place (forum). Gateways impact lives (Proverbs 31:23).

OVERCOMING THE PYTHON SPIRIT (DIVINATION):

Throughout this book we will focus on Acts 16:16, which specifically addresses the demon in the servant girl that harassed Paul the apostle as, "a spirit, a python," one inspired by Apollo, the god worshipped at Pytho, Delphi.

It also points out that although the demon in her, spoke the truth, it only did so "mockingly" and that Paul delayed casting out this demon, perhaps due to the "peril" it would expose his mission team to.

According to the footnotes of The Passion Translation (16:16); "In the religious context of Greek mythology, she was an 'oracle' a medium who had the spirit of the gods speaking through her to foretell the future. The Python spirit was the epithet of Apollo, known as the Greek god of prophecy. An individual (often a young virgin) who became the oracle of Apollo was known as the Python, or Pythia."

THE DIVINE MISSION
IS ALWAYS TO REVEAL CHRIST

The Holy Spirit always makes way for the rhema word of God to transform lives. Whereas the goal of religious witchcraft is always to stop our **effectiveness**, (our top mission being to reveal Christ to the world at large), which is accompanied by powerful prayer. "The prayer of a righteous man is powerful and **effective**." "The earnest (heartfelt, continued) prayer of a righteous man makes tremendous power available [dynamic in its working]" (James 5:16 AMPC). The word "effectiveness" is preferred to "success," (and less ego-centric).

These are the words of the Holy One, the True One, He who has the key [to the house] of David, *He who opens and no one will [be able to] shut, and He who shuts and no one*

18

opens... See, I have set before you an open door which no one is able to shut...

Revelation 3:7-8 AMP

Apostolically speaking, strategic doors or gates can only be opened by the leading of the Holy Spirit, which no one is able to shut. Equally speaking, when He shuts them no one is able to open. This is because God Himself opens or closes such doors. Doors of authority must be dealt with legally (not illegally — only Satan is the lawless one — 2 Thessalonians 2:8-9). God does everything by the book, He is righteous and just.

The apostolic ministry, has been singled out to deal with doors on this higher level; "that God may open a door..." doors may differ but the goal stays the same, "...for our message, **so that we may proclaim the mystery of Christ**" (Colossians 4:3 NIV). This is the sole agenda. The divine mission is always to reveal Christ.

The rhema word of God must be released powerfully and effectively by the apostolic ministry — with authority — and it must be spoken at strategic gates. "Her husband is known in the gates, when he sitteth among the elders of the land" (Proverbs 31:23 KJV).

HE USES THE APOSTOLIC MINISTRY:

So, as such strategic gate-keepers, apostles are tasked with the responsibility of opening or closing doorways/gateways for the mystery of Christ to be made known, far and wide (regions, cities, countries and nations). They operate and co-operate in arenas of greater authority than the average believer, as we will discuss throughout this book. Clearly not everyone is called to be an apostle; who are sent by Jesus who is Himself our, "Apostle and High Priest" (see Hebrews 3:1-6).

> Therefore, holy brothers and sisters, who share in the heavenly calling, [thoughtfully and attentively] consider the **Apostle and High Priest** whom we confessed [as ours when we accepted Him as Saviour], namely, **Jesus**; He was faithful to Him who appointed Him [Apostle and High Priest], as Moses also was faithful in all God's house.
>
> Yet Jesus has been considered worthy of much greater glory and honour than Moses, just as the **builder** of a house has more honour than the house. For every house is **built** by someone, but **the builder of all things is God.**
>
> Now Moses was faithful in [the administration of] all God's house, [but only] as a ministering servant, [his ministry serving] as a testimony of the things which were to be spoken afterward [the revelation to come in Christ]; but Christ is faithful as a Son over His [Father's] house. And we are His house if we hold fast our confidence and sense of triumph in our hope [in Christ].
>
> Hebrews 3:1-6 AMP

FOUNDATION BUILDERS:

The emphasis on **building** in the above passage of scripture is because apostles are **builders**, Christ is the master **builder** and the corner stone (see 1 Corinthians 3:10; Ephesians 2:20; 1 Peter 2:6). Specifically apostles are foundational, meaning their work for the kingdom of God is valid and can be built upon; also that which is built is long lasting. It doesn't expire or evaporate with the trends.

Ephesians 2:20 declares very clearly, **"built on the foundation of the apostles and prophets,** with Christ Jesus the chief cornerstone." So it is clear that the foundations of God's house are built on the apostles and prophets.

> Consequently, you are no longer foreigners and strangers, but fellow citizens with God's people and also **members of his household, built on the foundation of the apostles and prophets, with Christ Jesus himself as the chief cornerstone.** In him the whole building is joined together and rises to become a holy temple in the Lord. And in him you too are being built together to become a dwelling in which God lives by his Spirit.
>
> Ephesians 2:19-22 NIV

THE RESTORATION OF THE APOSTOLIC WAS ALWAYS GOD'S PLAN

The restoration of the apostolic is something I have been preaching (or banging on about) for decades now. I was called to be an apostle before I even understood the concept (what it really meant) and certainly before it was widely acceptable to speak of publicly. Few were open about it, like today.

In fact, it was really quite unpopular! And most folks were just getting to grips with the prophetic ministry (and the Joshua generation of the 1990s) and were still only comfortable calling everyone in ministry "pastor" (regardless of gifting).

Largely this was to do with the prevailing ignorance at the time, and those of us who were not late to the party were prophetically proclaiming it in advance. Once it is mainstream, it is much easier for people in general to tolerate and discuss.

But for a long time there was much resistance and an almost complete disregard for the fivefold ministry – let alone the apostolic – clearly not everyone can be called pastor!

But those of us who understood the movement of the apostolic restoration, knew that this was the last of the five fold ministries to be restored to the body of Christ – before Christ returned. People like Dr Bill Hamon and others, were great sources of encouragement in those days.

The apostolic ministry with signs following, always demonstrates more power (1 Corinthians 2:4-5) and causes a stronger "reaction" (Acts 16:16). This can be both positive and negative. At the close of the book of Acts, the account of what happened to Paul on the Island of Malta is a good example:

> In the vicinity of that place there were estates belonging to the leading man of the island, named Publius, who welcomed and entertained us hospitably for three days. And it happened that the father of Publius was sick [in bed] with recurring attacks of fever and dysentery; and Paul went to him, and after he had prayed, he laid his hands on him and healed him.
>
> After this occurred, the rest of the people on the island who had diseases were coming to him and being healed. They also gave us many honours [gifts and courtesies expressing respect]; and when we were setting sail, they supplied us with all the things we needed.
>
> Acts 28:7-10 AMP

NOT SO LOCAL:

So, it's safe to say that nothing was quiet and "local" for someone like Paul. Yet, apostles don't work alone. Also they know how to function in conjunction with the other gifts and can themselves operate in all gifts when necessary. And because Paul was the one to deal with this spirit of python, it is important to include teaching on the apostolic ministry. Not everyone deals with spirits on this level, which disrupt vast regions and stir up such toxic strife. But God knows who his big guns are!

APOSTLES GOD'S GATEKEEPERS

Finally, if you want the doors of blessing opened in your entire region or area (not just in your church), then it's time to invite the apostolic ministries in. They are the ones God used in scripture and uses them still today; for opening closed spiritual doors. For example if your area feels closed, no matter what you try and do, no matter how much you pray and fast, then you know what you must do.

They help "keep" spiritual doors or gates open too. Their office of anointing ensures that the anointing can flow through. It's not about them, but about what God wants to do through them. Once the doors are open, the move of the Spirit can flow into a region and do what only God can do.

Many times churches are closed and disconnected. There is no victory in isolation. Sanctification involves a degree of separation from the world, but not from the church. A dismembered body is not the body of Christ. Therefore, many local churches need to experience some form of "realignment"and reconnection with the rest of the body so that the right gifts can flow in and stand at the gates of the city, region, or nation and bring lasting change.

Gates will open to the right gifts, their purpose is to flood that area with the rhema word of God and to the flow of the Holy Spirit.

Which in turn brings a flow of blessing that will otherwise be very difficult to obtain. Pray today and ask God to help you invite the right gifts into your region, to help you open the right gates. The python tried to stop Paul. But ultimately couldn't, because he was God's tool for the job.

IT TAKES AUTHORITY TO DEAL WITH AUTHORITY

There is an organised nature to the structure of authority, (both in the physical or spiritual realms). And we must be organised and prepared before dealing with levels of authority. In other words it takes authority, to deal with authority.

There is a hierarchy of spiritual authority, similar to how an army or police force is constructed. For example where authority is distributed between local officers and higher-ranking officials. Authority is either local or regional, so there are local officers or precinct commanders, (with a broader jurisdiction). Like district level authorities; federal or special task forces, which oversee larger operations, for example.

The top tier of authority however is represented by high ranking generals or commissioners. Needless to say, the more authority one possesses — the more is achieved. Again, apostles are the big guns (according to rank and file). Not everyone can do what they do. The assignment on their lives is NOT GENERIC.

For the sake of balance its also important to point out here, that although excesses and imbalances have gotten into the apostolic ministry at various junctures in church history, it doesn't change the truth of God's word. He uses who He chooses and if we want to be effective (in a wider scope of authority and jurisdiction), then we must work together with God's elect apostles.

RAY MCCAULEY SOUTH AFRICA

The apostolic ministry is not to be feared or obsessively revered in any wrong way, (just the mention of apostles make some people nervous). While true apostles possess a higher level of authority, they are also true servants of Christ and His body.

One example is the late Pastor Ray McCauley who is known for his leadership in South Africa. After returning from bible school in the United States Ray founded Rhema Bible Church in Johannesburg, which grew rapidly into one of the largest congregations in South Africa. He was a key apostolic figure during those times. And had a reputation for his strong sense of authority.

Throughout his tenure he was a prominent public figure (involved in various social and charitable initiatives, focusing on humanitarian efforts and community development). But most importantly he was known for his efforts in promoting unity and dialogue among different communities during the turbulent times of apartheid.

These were volatile times indeed and is when his apostolic ministry was on full display. I believe God used Ray instrumentally during that crucial juncture in history, and it is widely accepted that his work greatly contributed to the social change and reconciliation efforts in that country. Clearly not all pastors work on that level.

PUT THIS TOOL IN THEIR HANDS

Finally dear reader, I know you will greatly enjoy this book and if you are in ministry or just starting out in ministry and can relate to the truths in this book, then pass along to someone who needs it; who perhaps is dealing with the same set of issues. (It can be such a relief when you realise you're not isolated).

Be your brother or sister's keeper and put this tool in their hands. Or consider going a step further and buying a bundle of copies for the purpose of opening up your home or church, for group study.

Note: For more insight (in connection with the subject covering the python spirit), also consider reading my book titled, **Seduction & Control Infiltrating Society and the Church**, ISBN 9781909132009.

❖

CHAPTER 1

The Python Spirit

DIVINATION & FALSE PROPHECY

It is some years now that I've been looking into what scripture calls, "the python spirit." And as we have just read in the introduction to this book, apostles are the major door openers, for the rhema word of God to flow into a territory. They have a wider impact than most and the python spirit is out to stop them and the rhema word that the Holy Spirit wants to reveal through them.

WITH THIS IN MIND LET'S BREAK IT DOWN:

> One day, as we were going to the house of prayer, we encountered a young slave girl who had an **evil spirit of divination, the spirit of Python.** She had earned great profits for her owners by being a fortune-teller.
>
> Acts 16:16 TPT

It came to pass in our going on to prayer, a certain maid, **having a spirit of Python,** did meet us... YLT

As with these two translations above, the Authorised Version also calls this spirit "python." However, not every translation available today, addresses it by this name and just uses "divination" instead.

THE GREEK FOR DIVINATION IS "PYTHON"

Strong's Number G4436–Πύθων. Transliterated as Puthōn (with the phonetic spelling *poo'-thone).*

STRONG'S DEFINITION:

From Πυθώ Puthō (the name of the region where Delphi the seat of the famous oracle was located); a Python that is (by analogy with the supposed diviner there) inspiration (soothsaying): - divination.

THAYER'S DEFINITION:

In Greek mythology the name of the Pythian serpent or dragon that dwelt in the region of Pytho at the foot of Parnassus in Phocis, and was said to have guarded the oracle at Delphi and been slain by Apollo. A spirit of divination.

When one looks up the literal purpose of divination, it's all about *access;* whether into individual lives or into entire territories, (cities, regions and nations). As we see in Acts 16 that a python spirit was trying to stop Paul's mission of introducing the gospel (for the first time), into Europe. So this was a significant confrontation, at a significant spiritual gateway. But Paul and his crew—led by the Holy Spirit—were up for the task.

CHRIST'S APOSTOLIC GATEKEEPERS

In parallel, the same is true of the apostolic ministry, which creates *access* for the rhema message of Christ and its power to flow into entire territories, (individual hearts, homes, towns, cities, regions and nations).

The apostolic ministry—through the global body of Christ the Church—is endued with the power of the Holy Spirit, since Pentecost. With the divine purpose of unveiling and revealing, "before every throne and rank of angelic orders in the heavenly realm God's full and diverse wisdom" (Ephesians 3:10 TPT).

Or, as the Amplified says, "So now through the church the multifaceted wisdom of God [in all its countless aspects] might now be made known [revealing the mystery] to the [angelic] rulers and authorities in the heavenly places" (AMP).

In this context, the Church of Jesus Christ, serves as the most important spiritual "gateway" in all of creation, especially for this planet, "For God so [greatly] loved and dearly prized the world..." (John 3:16 AMP)

PYTHON—LESS SEXUAL THAN JEZEBEL:

The python however sets out to "stranglehold" this apostolic (authoritative) preaching of the word, so that demonic (strongholds) can use spiritual "gateways" instead (I will continue breaking this down).

A python spirit is similar to that of a Jezebel minus the sexual overtones. For example, Jezebel is often associated with manipulation, control, seduction, immorality and rebellion. She was ultra super-spiritual too; remember she was a false prophetess. She represented idolatry and false worship.

The python spirit on the other hand operates less around sexual seduction and centralises on spiritual activities such as prophesy, prayer and especially targeting those with strategic positions (and greater degrees of spiritual authority), like those in the apostolic ministry.

This makes sense since God's household has been "...built on the foundation of the apostles and prophets," (Ephesians 2:20 NIV). And Satan's overall target is Christ's body but the GATES OF HELL will not prevail (Matthew 16:18).

PYTHON WENT AFTER THE WHOLE APOSTOLIC TEAM:

Notice however, that although Paul was the overall leader of that missionary team, there were other godly men present. She targeted them collectively saying, "These men are servants of the most high God." So she didn't just single Paul out, yet it was Paul who got vexed the most by her mocking and taunting.

We know that Paul was greatly annoyed, yet he still took his time, (only Satan's in a rush), the Holy Spirit is never "anxious" or "worked-up." BUT, I must point out here that the Greek word for "grieved" means exactly that: "worried, offended; to be worked up" (Strong's G1278).

Billy Graham is often widely quoted as saying that **"God cannot use a discouraged man."** I will take this a step further and say that God cannot use angry men either. It clouds our vision. So although it seems that this slave girl was really starting to get under Paul's skin; Paul did not verbally attack her or even rush the situation. People are often puzzled at his delayed reaction. Spiritual maturity looks to be led by the Holy Spirit and respond, rather than react in the flesh.

HOW PYTHON OPERATES TODAY:

Python was trying to get Paul into a mess, yet Paul will have been waiting for the right moment to cast that spirit out of her. In other words this was not a fleshly reaction that we saw from Paul, as we know that she was successfully delivered (you can't minister to people you don't love).

As our adversary is a master-strategist and legalist, let's look at the order, pattern and strategy with which the demon spirit python went to work in Acts chapter 16, (how it operated back then, is just how it operates today).

Satan has no new tricks. Ecclesiastes 1:9 says, "That which has been is that which will be [again], And that which has been done is that which will be done again. So there is nothing new under the sun" (AMP).

THE SIGNIFICANCE OF PRAYER

As the python spirit targeted Paul and the others, on their way to prayer, let's look at the significance of prayer. Remembering that praying is engaging in the unseen things of God, (and unbelief cannot pray).

PRAYER: (LIKE UNSEEN POWERFUL RADIATION)

I want to briefly liken prayer to radio waves, that cannot be seen by the naked eye, but are still very powerful and impactful.

Radio waves are a type of electromagnetic radiation, like visible light, but they have much longer wavelengths, which makes them invisible to us. Our eyes are only sensitive to a narrow range of wavelengths, which we perceive as colours.

So just imagine all the things that our eyes don't see. Thoughts exist, but you can't tangibly see them. Words also (unless we put them down on paper or into film etc). However, I believe that if we could see our praise and worship or our prayer language, we'd be amazed!

So, for a moment think of your prayers as electromagnetic radiation, (waves of energy that travel through space at the speed of light!) Think along the spectrum of: microwaves, radio waves, infrared, visible light, ultraviolet, X-rays and even gamma rays! Each type has different wavelengths and tremendous energy.

Our prayers also possess tremendously powerful energy, (although we can't see them with the naked eye) they still travel through space. Think of Daniel in chapter 10. His answer took 21 days to arrive, yet his request was answered (and released to him) from the very first day. That was fast!

Then he said to me, "Do not be afraid, Daniel, for **from the first day** that you set your heart on understanding this and on humbling yourself before your God, your words were heard, and *I have come in response to your words.* But the prince of the kingdom of Persia was standing in **opposition to me for twenty-one days.** Then, behold, Michael, one of the chief [of the celestial] princes, came to help me, for I had been left there with the kings of Persia.

Now I have come to make you understand what will happen to your people in the latter days, for the vision is in regard to the days yet to come."

Daniel 10:12-14 AMP

The battle that raged over Persia—was to try and prevent the rhema (revealed sayings) of God. Daniel prayed for revelation/understanding (Daniel chapters 8-9; 9:22). We must also pray for our territories; for our mission and assignments. This is why Paul and his group were praying. As mentioned in the introduction, Europe was being introduced to the gospel (rhema) for the very first time and they needed the continued guidance of the Holy Spirit. The divine executive.

PAUL & HIS TEAM WERE ON THEIR WAY TO PRAY

In verse 16 it says, **"...we were on our way to a place of prayer,"** this clearly shows that this spirit was very much interested in and attracted to effective intercession, (especially those who have weight in the spirit and a purpose to achieve). Satan won't waste his time chasing a storm in a tea-cup.

So the python spirit's first target is to infiltrate prayer groups, such as Paul's missionary team. It's goal is to disrupt effectiveness and prevent "great power" being made "available," (see James 5:16 AMP). Clearly such prayer is always going to pose a threat because it always gets the job done.

Daniel was one among many other servants of God in the Old Testament who were effective in prayer and who experienced grave opposition. However, his answer came regardless. And Jesus taught that we must persevere in prayer and not yield to the resistance — rather expect it (Luke 18:1-5). In other words, just like every other biblical example we could find — we too will be effective regardless — and must not be deterred or distracted by the spiritual resistance that we face.

EFFECTIVE REGARDLESS OF THE OPPOSITION:

Usually any person channelling a python spirit, loves to be at the centre of such prayer meetings, to elevate themselves as being highly spiritual and knowledgeable (this is a super spiritual pretence and ploy). In reality they say all the right things but are totally off base and it takes real discernment to call them out.

On this particular point the Life Application Study Bible says the following, (Acts 16:17) "What the slave girl said was true, although the source of her knowledge was a demon. **Why did a demon announce the truth about Paul, and why did this annoy Paul?** In the spiritual world, demons and angels are actively at war. Demons fight to drag as many people away from God as they can and to diminish the image of God in each person. They know God exists and has the power to destroy them."

PULLING DOWN FALSE PROPHECY:

It goes on to say, "If Paul accepted the demon's words, he would appear to be linking the Good News with demon-related activities. Satan always seeks to twist the truth of God's Word. Allowing the slave girl's demon to keep announcing their purpose would damage the communication of Paul's message about Christ. Truth and lies from Satan do not mix."

Although, this young slave girl had an evil spirit, and was clearly being exploited, there was still a responsibility on Paul to address these demonically-prophetic-outbursts; that were seeking to derail their mission from God.

Prophecy can be seen as either foretelling or telling-forth and this demon was making proclamations into the atmosphere (and it was not being discrete). 2 Corinthians 10:4-6 tells us to pull such things down:

> The weapons of our warfare are not physical [weapons of flesh and blood]. Our weapons are divinely powerful for the destruction of fortresses. *We are destroying sophisticated arguments and every exalted and proud thing that sets itself up against the [true] knowledge of God,* and we are taking every thought and purpose captive to the obedience of Christ, being ready to punish every act of disobedience, *when your own obedience [as a church] is complete."* AMP

This also ties nicely with the scripture found in James 4:17 saying, "Submit to [the authority of] God. Resist the devil [stand firm against him] and he will flee from you" (James 4:7 AMP). I must point out an important caveat here, for those who don't already know, that there are strongholds of the mind.

Our thoughts — which influence our actions — must obey God too (see Philippians 4:6-8). And our minds must not wander out of God's presence. Faith without actions is dead, but that doesn't mean that only outward actions are constituted as obedience. Because unbelief is the sin of the heart. While mere mental-assent is never enough and not equal to obedience — obedience does originate — from the inner man. So it is vital that our inner man is in order.

MISSION ACCOMPLISHED:

Going back to James 4:7; the Holy Spirit cannot be defeated. So, as we resist the demonic, God promises that it will flee from us. There is no peace for the demonic, in our presence, because we are submitted and with the power of the Holy Spirit, we are well able to overcome (Revelation 12:10-12).

In the Old Testament, God spoke to Jeremiah and said, "See! Today I have imparted to you great authority over nations and governments, to uproot and demolish, to destroy and dismantle. And you will plant and build something new" (Jeremiah 1:10 TPT).

Intuitively there has to be a pulling down (of the bad) before something better can replace it. Paul's mission to build and to plant the kingdom of God in Europe, was being threatened and potentially hijacked; he couldn't allow that — regardless of the repercussions — his devotion to the mission and his obedience to Christ, was all important (see Acts 16:6-10; also 9:15-16).

POSSESSING THE GATES OF THE ENEMY

Likewise, let's look now at our responsibility in and around prayer; we must also protect the mission that God has called us to (which the python still wants to disrupt Acts 16:10).

Prayer is just as necessary now as it was then. Paul's posse **"...were on their way to a place of prayer."** Prayer is never obsolete. Prayer in the life of our Saviour was equally as uncompromising, "Jesus Himself would often slip away to the wilderness and pray [in seclusion]" (Luke 5:16 AMP).

In other words, he habitually "withdrew," as the Greek implies here.

Cindy Jacobs in her book, Possessing the Gates of the Enemy, says, "History belongs to the intercessors." She goes on to quote Paul Billheimer as saying, "The church holds the balance of power in world affairs. ... Even now, in this present throbbing moment, by means of her prayer power and the extent to which she uses it, the praying church is actually deciding the course of human events."[1]

Obviously, this is not a spectator sport. So let's take another look at a lengthier excerpt taken from chapter 16 of Cindy Jacob's book, which specifically deals with enemy gates. As follows:

1. Discernment Point Number One:

The first thing to remember when finding the spiritual strongholds of a city is to be led by the Holy Spirit. God has a plan for each city. You cannot simply duplicate what has been done somewhere else. The strategy God has for your city can be obtained only through fasting and prayer. You must also determine the legal entrances that have allowed Satan to establish the strongholds in the first place.

These could be called the gates of the city... gates were strategic to the welfare of cities in biblical times. The city gates were symbols of authority. It was here that the elders met to discuss the welfare of the city and governmental issues. Satan works hard to gain entrance to cities. The gates that open to him do so because of the sin of people in the cities.

Once he can legally enter the city through sin or a "gate of hell," he moves in and out freely.

The city does not have to be lost forever. Matthew 16:18 gives us a precious promise concerning this, "On this rock I will build My church, and the gates of Hades shall not prevail against it" (NKJV). When we found our cities on God's laws or reclaim them according to those laws, then the gates of hell cannot prevail.

There are other beautiful promises in Scripture concerning gates. One of these is Isaiah 28:6, "And... strength to those who turn back the battle at the gate" (NKJV). God will be our strength as we battle the enemy at the gates of our city. Another one is found in Genesis 22:17, "And your descendants shall possess the gate of their enemies" (NKJV).

As we are faithful to the Lord, He will raise up our descendants, or "our seed" as some translations say, to possess the gate of the enemy.

2. Discernment Point Number Two:

In order to close Satan's gate into the city, we must discover the sins of the city. Then we must repent of these sins to stop his kingdom from ruling. Sin must be repented of corporately because the sin is corporate. This is not always an easy concept for Americans to grasp. You might ask, "But it isn't my sin. Aren't those people responsible for what they have done before God?" Of course they are. But God judges cities as a whole.

Look at the judgment of God that fell on Babylon and other wicked cities. Cities do not have eternal souls so they must receive their judgment in the here and now.

We as intercessors stand in the gap for our cities and cry, "In judgment remember mercy. We deserve judgment, but please spare us." Each person in the city will someday stand before God for his or her individual sin, but we can still repent for a city or nation and ask God to forgive it as a whole.

Remember that Daniel stood in the gap for the sins of his nation even though he was righteous, "We have sinned and committed iniquity, we have done wickedly and rebelled, even by departing from Your precepts and Your judgments" (Daniel 9:5 NKJV).

Nehemiah also repented of the sins of his people, "We have acted very corruptly against You, and have not kept the commandments, the statutes, nor the ordinances which You commanded Your servant Moses" (Nehemiah 1:7 NKJV).

Actually, humankind has territorial dominion. Adam was told to tend the Garden of Eden even though a whole world existed. The disciples were given specific directions of strategy for possession of the kingdom.

You and I are, in a sense, "territorial spirits" because it is God who chooses when we will be born and, if we are following Him, where we will live. He has destined us to be in certain places geographically to possess the gates of the enemy in the land.

How do you discover the sins against God in your city? Begin by looking at the three areas where Satan establishes his rulership: Physical, spiritual and political.

You may well uncover ungodliness in each area. Do research through books written about the city or the nation.

Talk to local historians and those who have lived in the community for many years. I am convinced that God has set aside people for the task of researching the city's history whether or not they realise it.

Here is a list of questions we use when we research cities for Generals International:

- Why was the city established? Is there any indication of corruption in government?

- Who were the first people who lived in the area and what happened to them?

- What does the city say about itself? Any slogans or mottos?

- What were the principles upon which the city was established? Were those who organised the government godly or corrupt?

- Who introduced Christianity into the area? Is there any evidence of religious deception?

- Has the city, or its people, ever suffered any type of physical disaster? Any evidence of traumas that would affect the whole community?

- Is there any evidence of greed in the economic system?

You can also find evidence of demonic influence by studying the music, culture, architecture and art. **Many times visible things are clues to the invisible realm.**[2]

For ever since the creation of the world His invisible attributes, His eternal power and divine nature, have been clearly seen, being understood through His workmanship [all His creation, the wonderful things that He has made], so that they [who fail to believe and trust in Him] are without excuse and without defence.

For even though they knew God [as the Creator], they did not honour Him as God or give thanks [for His wondrous creation]. On the contrary, they became worthless in their thinking [godless, with pointless reasonings, and silly speculations], and their foolish heart was darkened. Claiming to be wise, they became fools, and exchanged the glory and majesty and excellence of the immortal God for an image [worthless idols] in the shape of mortal man and birds and four-footed animals and reptiles.

Romans 1:20- 23 AMP

❖

CHAPTER 2

Mammon & Flattery

EXPLOITATIVE, GREEDY AND CORRUPT

So, in the previous chapter, we looked at how python targets prayer and those in strategic positions of leadership (both then and now). To continue, let's look at other avenues namely money, greed and flattery; usual staples for those seeking position and power.

Recollect that this slave girl was being pimped — groomed and trafficked — as we'd say in our modern day vernacular and she was making a killing (Acts 16:16). In other words, she was turning a lucrative profit; something her owners were loath to see the back of.

What a ruckus they made once they discovered their, "hope of profit was gone" (16:19, 22). The word "gone" is so final. They realised their money-cow had finally stopped producing and their golden goose had permanently stopped laying eggs, (see chapter 19:28-34 when Paul upset another mob for confronting idolatry in Ephesus, who kicked-up a riot in defence of "Artemis/Diana" lasting two straight hours).

However on this particular occasion, not only were these "pimps" exploitative, greedy and corrupt, they were totally ignorant. They had zero concept that their slave was already under ownership (by the devil), and the spirit controlling her had a whole other agenda than lining their pockets. To prevent the gospel reaching Europe (too late!)

The Holy Spirit had prevented Paul and his crew from reaching Turkey and had them reach Northern Greece instead, so it was already determined. The gospel had already reached its shores and Lydia (who was influential) had already received the good news. Then the jailor and his entire family. The fire of the gospel message was already burning.

DISCERNMENT IS NECESSARY:

So, up to this juncture, Python had used this girl to corrupt many minds and hearts using false prophecy, lies, deception and greed. Such are the surrounding factors. (As mentioned before, nothing has changed). Look for the signs. Recognise its evil legacy today, "Ye shall know them by their fruits ...a corrupt tree bringeth forth evil fruit" (Matthew 7:16-17 KJV).

Therefore we can see plainly that this spirit uses greed (the love of money), extreme narcissism (the need for attention, exposure and recognition), appetite for position (uses strategy to gain access to the top/proximity to leadership).

Finally, it is ultra needy to impress with its bold super-spirituality and shameless-flattery. It was restless, relentless and insatiable, (which can be misinterpreted as spiritual hunger).

THE DEFINITION OF MAMMON

By definition, mammon represents an intense, excessive desire for wealth and material possessions. It's often linked to greed, selfishness, and an unhealthy attachment to money. In many religious and philosophical teachings, mammon is considered a symbol of idolatry, where the pursuit of wealth takes priority over spiritual or moral values. In Christianity especially, mammon is seen as idolatrous. This is the link with witchcraft (divination).

Loving money leads ultimately to disobedience, moral failure, spiritual corruption and a complete disconnect from calling and divine purpose (see 1 Samuel 15:23; Romans 8:28).

He has a morbid interest... corrupted in mind and deprived of the truth, *who think that godliness is a source of profit [a lucrative, money-making business—withdraw from them].*

But godliness actually is a source of great gain when accompanied by contentment... *But those who [are not financially ethical and] crave to get rich [with a compulsive, greedy longing for wealth] fall into temptation* and a trap and into many foolish and harmful desires that plunge people into ruin and destruction [leading to personal misery].

For the love of money [that is, the greedy desire for it and the willingness to gain it unethically] is a root of all sorts of evil, and some by longing for it have wandered away from the faith and pierced themselves [through and through] with many sorrows.

see all of 1 Timothy 6:3-10 AMP

HOW TRUE MEN OF GOD REACT TO FLATTERY:

Also consider the flattery it used and the false display of loyalty it showed towards the truth, "...they are proclaiming to you the way of salvation!" In verse 17 it says she "...kept following Paul and [the rest of] us" (AMPC).

She was persistent. Anything tormenting usually is and people operating with this spirit "attach" themselves to men and women of God. However, their allegiance is false (due to hidden agendas and ambitions). Meaning that it is all about them and what they can get out of the situation and not about the mission of God.

Evidently, this is why Paul was so angry, because he was mission-oriented and didn't want his focus pulled in other directions. Likewise, all leaders with a mission from God — get harassed relentlessly — especially when they are being effective. The enemy wants to shut them down.

THE WHOLEHEARTED NATURE OF AN APOSTLE

Wholeheartedness is a characteristic of true leadership. They are all in. And at times our prominent leaders don't seem to catch a break, because the enemy deliberately seeks to wear them out.

In fact anyone in ministry knows just how exhausting, wearying, fatiguing, draining, sapping, stressful, trying, crushing; demanding, exacting, taxing, challenging, burdensome, arduous, gruelling, punishing, grinding, strenuous and uphill, that ministry life can be! It is not glamorous. The devil is banking on it (see Galatians 6:9; Luke 9:62).

This is precisely why Paul had to put an end to it. Not necessarily because Paul was being cowardly or self-preservational — after all she was just a servant girl.

Seriously speaking, Paul's reliable track record proved otherwise; both his life and his death, spoke volumes about his unwavering sense of commitment; to the Jesus he met on the Damascus Road (Acts 9:3-10).

Rather, we came to know apostle Paul as a selfless human being. So, in keeping with his known character, Paul was more about preserving the mission and his fellow companions, than his own feelings or wellbeing. Consider it; having his team or delegation exhausted (spiritually drained) would have served no purpose nor aided their assignment at all.

NOTHING COULD COMPROMISE THE MISSION:

Therefore, no matter how reluctant Paul seemed, (to cast the spirit out of the girl), this could have been for a combination of reasons. One, simply of avoiding stirring up needless strife, which could potentially have cut their mission short.

Actually, things could have gotten messy — either way — and those of us in ministry know that keeping the peace comes with much conflict sometimes. It can't always be avoided. Although we seek to keep the peace (and be peace makers), sometimes keeping the mission intact must be our first order of priority; (what you compromise to keep, you lose anyway). So, I'm convinced this was Paul's mind-set, rather than an emotional one.

By all written accounts (on record), it was impossible to get someone like Paul, off track. Re-visit 2 Corinthians 11:22-33, where Paul gives an exhaustive list of all the trials he faced for the sake of the gospel.

Undeterred — even in the face of death — Paul shared Christ's heart for the early church; desperately wanting spiritual maturity to be formed in them, "Besides those external things there is the daily [inescapable] pressure of my concern for all the churches..." (v28, AMP)

AN APOSTOLIC MINDSET NEVER TAKES VACATIONS:

Paul recognised that such fixed determination was supernatural and not a result of his flesh. He took no glory for the call and gifts on his life (the apostolic office of anointing). He would say, in acknowledgment of this: "That's why I work and struggle so hard, depending on Christ's mighty power that works within me." (Colossians 1:29 NLT). Or, "...with his power flowing through me" (TPT).

Now I rejoice in my sufferings on your behalf... In this church *I was made a minister according to the stewardship which*

God entrusted to me for your sake, so that I might make the word of God fully known [among you]...

We proclaim Him, warning and instructing everyone in all wisdom [that is, with comprehensive insight into the word and purposes of God], *so that we may present every person complete in Christ [mature, fully trained, and perfect in Him—the Anointed]. For this I labour [often to the point of exhaustion], striving with His power and energy, which so greatly works within me.*

Colossians 1:24-29 AMP

Although Paul the apostle is unequalled, I can personally vouch for this apostolic mindset; we rarely turn-off. We don't think in terms of vacations, perks or even retirement (rather re-fire-ment!)

We are not workaholics (that's a humanistic approach), this is limited to the arm of the flesh and doing things in one's own strength. I speak more of the regular burdens we face and the weighty responsibilities involved in the call. Apostles "live" their labour of love, which seeks tirelessly for the full maturing of the body of Christ, (see Colossians 1:24-29; 1 Thessalonians 2:9). It is an outward — not inward — burden.

FALSE LOYALTIES & INDISCRETIONS:

In the passing of time these individuals who channel this spirit of python, often create a false sense of security around leaders; giving the impression of 100% loyalty, while simultaneously causing them great personal "distress." Everything sounds right, they have all the right-words to say, but like someone once said, *"it's just like trying to wash your feet with your socks on..."* something just isn't right!

Then there is the loudness aspect to it, as seen in Acts 16:17 where it says she, "...kept screaming and shouting" (AMP). Those who operate like this lack a great deal of discretion. In fact these individuals are incapable of being sensitive to the Holy Spirit, although they seem very spiritual, (their behaviour is self-contradictory and conflicting).

They are loud and draw all the attention to themselves and away from what God's really doing (suck all the oxygen out of everything). They have the capacity to stir up a false atmosphere and a "forced-sense-of-excitement," which men of God with discernment can see through (as Paul did), but mostly others are influenced and distracted, which can jeopardise our effectiveness.

TEAM-BUILDING FOR THE MISSION FIELD

A WORD TO THE WISE:

If you are trying to build a team around yourself, (especially when new to ministry or your ministry is growing), you will quickly discover there's always one individual who— no matter what you say—will always draw others into the flesh, (into that carnal realm and away from the things of the Spirit). They like to show off and joke around and make everyone laugh.

This always seems to happen when you least want or need it—on the verge of some long-awaited breakthrough— suddenly those around you get distracted and lose focus.

Like being in the trenches during a battle—there's a time for everything—joking around at the wrong time can cost you everything.

It can be genuinely frustrating having a weak-link in your midst. BUT, always remember that it's *your* job to train them up! Teach them how to recognise such tactics and not to side with their own flesh or the weaknesses of others.

Evidently, if you fail to surround yourself with spiritual maturity (or train team members to be mature), you will face these kinds of issues regularly. You will also discover that the pressures of ministry, can draw out—the very best or worst—in those around you. Not everyone can cut it. Meaning not everyone can cope with the cost of full time ministry. Which is to deny their flesh daily (through basic sanctification) and stay focused long enough to get the job done.

NOT A WALK IN THE PARK

Then of course, you will find those who think themselves to already be spiritually mature and will openly compete for your position! It can get quite interesting striking the balance between the two—the weak-link who likes his/her flesh too much and the super spiritual one, who thinks they know best.

Paul the apostle faced such challenges, with difficult team members who abandoned them mid-assignment and left them in the lurch.

After some time Paul said to Barnabas, "Let us go back and visit the brothers and sisters (believers) in every city where we preached the message of the Lord, and see how they are doing." Now Barnabas wanted to take [his cousin] John, who was called Mark, along with them. But *Paul kept insisting that they should not take along with them the one who had quit and deserted them* in Pamphylia and had not gone on with them to the work.

And *it became such a sharp disagreement that they separated from one another,* and Barnabas took [John] Mark with him and sailed away to Cyprus. But Paul chose Silas [who was again in Antioch] and set out [on his second journey], commended by the brothers to the grace and favour of the Lord. And he traveled through Syria and Cilicia, strengthening the churches.

Acts 15:36-41 AMP

Notice how this division occurred just one chapter prior to the python encounter. Although, I must point out that this breach was eventually repaired—we see at a later juncture them working together again—the issue had been resolved or forgiven (see Colossians 4:10; Philippians 1:24; 2 Timothy 4:11).

Considering all the adventures Paul and Silas went through together on this particular missionary trip—traveling with someone like Paul, was not for the faint hearted or the delicate constitution!

They were seized/dragged/publicly stripped/beaten with rods and thrown into a high security prison. And if that wasn't enough, to cap things off they found themselves at the very epicentre of a very powerful earthquake (Acts 16:19, 22, 24, 25-26). What a climax!

Clearly not everyone is at the level of maturity required of them when they first start out and spiritual relationships are not a walk in the park. In fact, all of your relationships will be tested on the mission field, but this is *par for the course.* And any apostle worth their salt, will always demand high levels of spiritual maturity around them at all times, because you can't take spiritual babies into battle.

The ambitions or weaknesses of your own people — those closest to you and who walk with you in the ministry — can get in the way, even family members. (Jesus emphasised spiritual kinship over biological ties when using his own family as an example, see Matthew 12:48; Mark 3:33; Luke 8:21). Training others to be mission-oriented can be both rewarding and very tiring.

PYTHON'S GOAL IS TO TORMENT

So, to follow on from here, we know by now that those channeling this demon, are super spiritual and very annoying. BUT, we are not up against flesh and blood. See how Paul dealt with this situation, by speaking to the demon directly and not the girl, "Paul being grieved turned and said to the spirit..." (Acts 16:18 KJV) There is no record that he spoke to her at all.

To be clear verse 18 says, "...she said this for many days." Torment by its very nature is unrelenting; to the point that Paul and the others were "...sorely annoyed and worn out." This meant: *troubled, offended and worked up* (Gk1278 Strong's). This spirit's attempts were designed — then as now — to exhaust, tire out, weaken and drain leadership (especially those at the helm), as with Paul. Again, we can see how it grieved him the most, which was intentional.

❖

CHAPTER 3

Python is Territorial

A STUDY BORN OUT OF EXPERIENCE

Some time ago, after my wife and I "endured" similar circumstances in our own ministry, we decided to make a study of this spirit and its major manifestations. So this book is born out of experience; living and working in different countries and spiritual climates.

Once again — as repeated throughout this book — nothing changes in how it operates, all the "out-workings" are the same, even if the host person used by this spirit is different. Therefore its relevancy applies today.

Firstly, we found that if this "spirit" (python) is in operation in any area, then several major things occur:

confusion, distraction, diversion, rivalry, competition, gossip, slander and churches just being "incapable" of working together. And yes; all of this can go off in just one city, town or place.

In fact if you are a leader and this is going on in your town, then you will find that this spirit will "stir up the people" (vehemently) against you.

Even others in leadership will get stirred up against you. Those relationships you thought were friendships and allies (who you could work together with) will completely fall apart. (Note: To pit leaders against each other is a special trophy. At this level of authority, it is most damaging to a city).

Now as mentioned, those operating in this python spirit like to demand all the attention but they also like to engage in lots of false prophecies (by declaring the opposite of what God is really saying). Therefore divination occurs (also see familiar spirits in 1 Samuel 28:7).

EFFECTING ALL THE PEOPLE

This spirit will affect everybody not just leaders, even though it goes mainly for the head honcho. Its influence is felt by everyone, especially if it gains a stronghold in an area. We saw this first hand in a region, it operated amongst the churches so strongly that eventually things just began to fall utterly apart. It did irreparable damage for some, and others are still trying to rebuild their lives.

It causes "madness" (making people question their own sanity) and causes people to "endlessly question" God's will for their lives (where previously people were generally secure and clear headed). It is when people feel that they have to constantly second-guess themselves, or justify themselves all the time, that things get very intense. And ultimately severe hopelessness sets in. Many in leadership give up the ministry and simply walk away.

This spirit also causes such "tiredness" a spiritual, extremely strong and overpowering tiredness; because all the mind games drain people of their vital spiritual energy.

Going back to "hopelessness" just briefly, this was one of the major oppressive elements that we discovered in a small town where we used to live. Also this spirit of python was in operation within the whole region making the churches there totally incapable of working together on any real level. And there existed an overriding sense of hopelessness amongst the people we had to minister to.

REGIONS WITH PROFOUND POTENTIAL:

The place offered profound potential. There was apparent wealth and opportunity and yet so many of the folks we ministered to there, were extremely affected by this deep sense of "hopelessness." On the surface an outsider would not detect it perhaps, but living there for some time, it became so obvious that the average person there was really suffering with it. Hope deferred really does make the heart sick.

What often followed in succession was deep depression and disappointments in people and this provoked much murmuring and gossip. In fact in an area where python has a stronghold, there will be MUCH murmuring, complaining and gossip. It affects everyone underneath its influence, but its target is especially at leaders.

Leaders end up feeling so tied-up that they can't move freely by the spirit as they want to. There is this overwhelming sense that they better "please" the people so that murmuring stops, but of course it doesn't. The plan of course is spiritual suffocation, which involves "emotional blackmailing" to exhaust, drain and zap the energy, both mentally and spiritually.

Python will drain leaders as with Paul, by sending people who appear to be "supportive" (of all their hard work and efforts) but actually challenge every decision and every move they make; usurping their authority by lifting up their own agenda or the ones who sent them!

KEEP THE APOSTOLIC OUT OF "OUR CITY"

Then comes the mockery; they try to overpower people by mocking them and showing outward disrespect. Every opinion they have is loud and public. They are extremely VERBAL and designed to be "intimidating." This makes people take sides with it, in fear of reprisal. No one confronts them.

Those who need all the attention for themselves permanently are probably operating with a python spirit. Now I am not talking about basic immaturity, which likes centre stage like a child does, but we are talking mainly about those who have influence around ministers and who operate in a premeditated manner especially against authority. (Note: it is a great victory to bring leaders down by making the people question their authority).

Essentially the python spirit takes people's focus and attention from the Lord and puts it on to other things; just as the slave girl did, who angered Paul so much. But why Paul? Paul was a gatekeeper and a gate opener. The demon in her was trying to prevent the spread of the good news in Europe and beyond.

It only managed to slow Paul down for a hot minute but ultimately didn't stop him/them. And in the meantime Lydia who was a business woman became the first convert in Europe; followed in quick succession by the jailer and his whole family (not to exclude all those prisoners who got front row seats to the praise and miracle show, Acts 16:25-26).

So, Paul successfully entered through this European GATE with a bang and once it was open, it would remain open (according to Revelation 3:7; 1 Corinthians 16:9; 2 Corinthians 2:12). And now it was open for all those who would come after them, to continue spreading the gospel; throughout successive generations.

PYTHON IS A TERRITORIAL SPIRIT:

The python spirit wants to rule and posses cities and entire regions, not just insignificant slave girls. Verse 20 says, "...OUR city." Python's agenda was the city, the region and beyond. It was not personal, it was opposition to the purpose of his mission. Paul and his companions didn't go home with their tails between their legs, they pressed through, for the sake of the gospel in that part of the world.

I will point out here that "Legion," didn't mind being cast out of the man and into a herd of pigs. BUT, it certainly didn't want to be cast out of that region; "He began BEGGING Him repeatedly not to send them out of the region..." (AMP) The region or territory was more of a concern (see Mark 5:1-20; Matthew 8:28-34; Luke 8:26-39).

Notice how, in verse 17, the people sided with the demonic; "...the people began to BEG with Jesus to leave THEIR REGION" (AMP). Therefore people in a region will side with (reflect or mirror) the spiritual sentiments or atmosphere of the ruling spirits over them, (until they hear the truth preached and are set free of such influence). This is why preaching the gospel has real power in any region.

Remember also, that Persia was a REGION, which was being governed by demonic powers. It too was violently repellent to divine revelation—rhema! (Daniel 10:13)

Back to Acts 16; if Paul's apostolic team could have been successfully infiltrated, then it would have shut them down (from advancing and being spiritually effective) and constrict their legitimate apostolic authority that had the power to silence and cast python out.

GATES: KEY CONTACTS & DIVINE CONNECTIONS

The first gate to open in Macedonia, once Paul's team landed, was Lydia. The spirit of python wants to stop networking by the Holy Spirit, which is essential to our task and so that God's will can be done on earth as it is in heaven.

We experienced this first hand. For example, my wife and I and our small children landed in Tuscany, Italy, with nowhere to go. God led us every step of the way. He supernaturally opened doors at every turn and connected us with all the right people. The same happened when we moved to Germany, during another season of our lives. God was always in control.

> While Paul shared the good news with her, God opened her heart to receive Paul's message. She devoted herself to the Lord, and we **baptised her and her entire family.** Afterward she urged us to stay in her home, saying, **"Since I am now a believer in the Lord, come and stay in my house."** So we were persuaded to stay there.
>
> Acts 16:14-15 TPT

WHY LYDIA WAS IMPORTANT:

Lydia was a gate. Her hospitality mattered. Gates can be both places and people. For example, God opened the door to the continent of Africa for my ministry, by using Pastor Tunde Bakare.

During a trip to London, he was given a copy of my book (The Reality of a Warrior); his response was to invite me to preach in his church, Latter Rain Assembly, in Lagos, Nigeria. After walking through that single door — in obedience — the whole of Africa opened up to me. Prior to that experience, I had never set foot in Africa! Now, everywhere I go — even in Europe — it's like Africa to me. So, he was a strategic door which God used three long decades ago. And what God opens, no man can close.

So what about Lydia? She was an influential business-woman and a Jewish convert. So she was already a worshipper of the God of Israel (but not yet a follower of Jesus until she met Paul) and was positioned ready to receive this missionary team. Following her conversion and baptism, she showed immense hospitality to this delegation sent by God.

Our first introduction to Lydia was in Acts 16:14; where she was amongst the first to meet Paul, and proved to be a providential connection in that region.

Specifically, she dealt with luxury items such as exquisite purple cloth, which in the ancient world was associated with the wealthy of society, even royalty. Because the dye used to create such purple fabric, came from a rare and expensive source, meaning that only those who could afford it, could wear it! (Her ties with the aristocracy would have been advantageous).

THE GOSPEL HAD TOUCHED-DOWN & LANDED:

Philippi was a major city, which python wanted to keep control of. It was a strategic place and will forever be marked as the first European city that heard the gospel preached by the Holy Spirit, in apostle Paul. This was a significant moment for the spread of Christianity and which laid a foundation for the early church in that territory.

LYDIA'S STORY HIGHLIGHTS A FEW IMPORTANT ISSUES:

The Holy Spirit doesn't just open gates and people, He keeps them open. He "sustains" them; using prominent divine connections and key supporters such as Lydia. Her ongoing support would have been invaluable.

Also God was not opposed to using prominent women, whose roles were pivotal. Individuals of various backgrounds can be used to help further the kingdom of God.

THE HOLY SPIRIT'S INCUBATION OF EUROPE (NOTHING HAPPENS IN A VACUUM)

Evidently the Holy Spirit was long brooding over Europe (incubating) much like He was during the account of creation—ready to bring LIFE—in Genesis 1:2. Nothing happens in a vacuum. He is always at work and we put our faith in the *unseen* things of God. Who works behind the scenes, setting the stage for the Father's will to be performed, changing nations and lives forever.

All of which the python spirit tried to hijack because once Lydia received salvation, the opposition began in earnest.

THE HOLY SPIRIT CAN'T BE DEFEATED:

Often referred to as a spiritually dark continent, because of its secularism, sophistication and skepticism, Europe today is still largely repellent to the gospel, but still can't stop its expansion within its borders.

Back then particularly, this spiritual gateway into the region of Macedonia was fiercely repellent yet — I repeat — the Holy Spirit won't be defeated and continues to use the apostolic to break down such gates today (like the "battle axe" of Jeremiah 51:20).

He is a master strategist and executive of the Godhead here on earth, through the Church. In other words, He knows what He's doing.

As a leading city in the region of Macedonia (and a Roman colony), Philippi was extremely strategic for divine plans. The Holy Spirit knew where to send Paul, and where not to send him. Using dreams to guide them:

> The Holy Spirit had forbidden Paul and his partners to preach the word in the southwestern provinces of Turkey... they repeatedly attempted to go north into the province of Bithynia, but again the Spirit of Jesus would not allow them to enter. So instead they went right on through the province of Mysia to the seaport of Troas.
>
> While staying there **Paul experienced a supernatural, ecstatic vision during the night. A man from Macedonia appeared before him, pleading with him, "You must come across the sea to Macedonia and help us!" After Paul had this vision, we immediately prepared to cross over to Macedonia, convinced that God himself was calling us to go and preach the wonderful news of the gospel to them...**
>
> Finally we reached **Philippi, a major city in the Roman colony of Macedonia,** and we remained there for a number of days.
>
> Acts 16:6-13 TPT

In just a matter of days, the territorial spirits of that region had stirred up such a fierce resistance, accusing Paul and his team of being, "troublemakers," who were "throwing **OUR CITY** into confusion" (16:20 TPT). But, by verse 39 Paul had them running scared, openly begging them, **"PLEASE LEAVE OUR CITY"!**

Paul knew who he was IN CHRIST (not just as a Roman citizen), but also as an apostle sent by God, with sovereign authority that superseded theirs.

THE GATES OF HELL DEFEATED IN MACEDONIA:

Because Paul came from a position of authority, he knew how to handle authority. That's the key. And verse 37 tells us that, "Paul told the officers, 'Look, they had us beaten in public, without a fair trial — and we are Roman citizens. Do you think we're just going to quietly walk away after they threw us in prison and violated all of our rights? **Absolutely not! You go back and tell the magistrates that they need to come down here themselves and escort us out!'"**

Paul certainly knew his place. In both realms! So python and every other territorial spirit involved knew that they had been defeated, which we see in verse 38, "...**the magistrates were frightened... and apologised** to Paul and Silas," begging them to leave! (Acts 16:38-39 TPT)

The reality was, a higher authority had come to town, leaving python defeated and reduced to cringing and fawning fear! So Paul and his counterparts were able to continue their mission undeterred. The entire affair highlighted God's power (especially v26).

As a side note, it is unclear why only Paul and Silas were targeted and thrown into prison, there is no account given as to what happened to the other members of the original missionary team who landed with Paul and Silas and we saw praying together (including Dr Luke the writer of the account and likely Timothy also, see Acts 16:10). It is considered probable by some, that it was because Paul and Silas were both prominent *Jews* (16:20), while the others were not. However, there is no mention that they were *abandoned* by their team, only that they were targeted by the mob.

WARNING TO THE CHURCHES

Finally, God has been speaking to me about the role of the apostolic; they are gatekeepers which also makes them door openers. They sustain the *access* too, meaning the doors remain open to allow the ministry of the Spirit and the word (rhema) to flow in, ensuring a move of God in the area. One must work with apostles, in order to be supernaturally effective on a higher level.

Many times churches are closed, they are not connected and they need realignment, so that the right gifts can stand at the gates of the city, region, or nation.

Gates will open to the right gifts, with the right level of authority. It takes the right spiritual keys to open the right spiritual doors (or the right spiritual biometrics!) They will bring a flow of blessing that will otherwise be very difficult to obtain. Pray for and invite the right gifts into your territory, to help you open the right doors. The python tried to stop Paul. But ultimately couldn't because he was God's man for the job.

Recognise who God is using today. Allow for divine connections and Holy Spirit networking, which must take place. This is His church. So look for those connections (as the Spirit leads) for they will bring the right flow into your church and ministry.

CHAPTER 4

Gateway into Europe

TAKING THE GOSPEL TO THE GRECO-ROMAN WORLD

However her masters weren't interested in harassing Paul—because there was nothing in it for them—in fact she even *lost* them money. Instead that *demonic spirit* locked target on Paul and his group—intent not to let go—until Paul put an end to it. The nature of a python is classified as a "constrictor." (Non-venomous snakes like the python rely on subduing their prey by coiling around it and squeezing to prevent breathing, leading to suffocation).

> She <u>kept following Paul and [the rest of] us, shouting loudly,</u>
> These men are the servants of the Most High God!
>
> Acts 16:17 AMPC

So, before we go any further let's look at the nature of a python in its natural habitat, to garner why this spirit operates like it does.

THE NATURE OF A PYTHON IN ITS NATURAL HABITAT

CONSTRICTION:

A python snake kills its prey primarily through constriction, a method in which the snake uses its muscular body to wrap around the prey and squeeze it tightly. Here's how the process works:

1. Ambush and Bite:

Pythons are non-venomous, so they rely on stealth to ambush their prey. When they strike, they use their sharp, curved teeth to latch onto the prey and hold it in place.

2. Constriction:

Once they have a firm grip with their teeth, the python quickly coils its body around the prey. Using powerful muscles, the python tightens its coils every time the prey exhales, preventing it from breathing.

3. Circulatory Arrest:

While it's commonly thought that constriction kills by suffocation, recent studies suggest that the primary cause of death is circulatory arrest. The intense pressure disrupts blood flow, causing the heart to stop and leading to a rapid loss of consciousness.

4. Swallowing:

Once the prey is dead, the python uncoils and begins swallowing it whole, headfirst. Pythons have highly flexible jaws and elastic skin, allowing them to consume prey much larger than their head.

Pythons typically prey on animals such as birds, mammals, and reptiles, depending on their size and habitat. The entire process, from constriction to swallowing, can take anywhere from a few minutes to several hours, depending on the size of the prey.

MY TAKE AWAY:

A non-venomous enemy can only rely on stealth and strong muscles to prevent breathing. In reference to, "intense pressure that disrupts blood flow," this reminds me of the vine, spoken of in John 15; if the spiritual sap stops flowing (Holy Spirit), spiritual death occurs. Our hearts stop beating for the Lord and we "rapidly" lose God consciousness.

When it "...tightens its coils every time we exhale," implies that each time we relax (or don't spend time inhaling God's presence or spending time in the secret place), that's when python capitalises most on our weaknesses. Yet, no spiritual "hit-job" can reach us in the secret place of the Most High (Psalm 91:1-4).

Headfirst, implies leadership first. And going after prey, "much larger than itself," implies that we have much more size and authority in the spirit realm than it does (legally), yet it attacks anyway. Indicating that it comes from the lawless one and does not fear undermining our legitimate authority — and will like a natural python — take its time dismantling its prey. (She harassed them for *days* and wouldn't have stopped until Paul made her).

THE RIGHT SPIRITUAL AUTHORITY
MUST BE ENFORCED

UNTIL rightful authority is enforced, it will just be ignored or scoffed at. Paul had to exercise (enforce) his spiritual authority to make python stop. Otherwise their mission was in danger of becoming sidetracked and aborted.

Think of it. **"The testimony of Jesus is the spirit of prophecy"** (Revelation 19:10 NKJV). Satan can only use false prophecy. The spirit of python spoke falsely, (this includes projecting right-sounding words, with a wrong spirit). So this was a direct clash between "false" and "true." We know truth prevailed because the girl was delivered from oppression and the gospel gained full access to the rest of Europe, just as the Holy Spirit had directed.

To be clear there is no equal-opposite correlation between true and false. In spite of this, the false will always reign until truth is enforced as the classic saying goes:

The only thing necessary for the triumph of evil is for good men to do nothing.

— Edmund Burke
(Irish Philosopher 18th Century)

Going back to the purpose of "constriction," this is used not just for restraining prey for ingestion (and so that it cannot escape), but also for self-defence, ensuring the snake won't get injured in the process.

Legally and spiritually, the snake (and his dominion) has already been fatally injured. "I will put enmity (open hostility) between you and the woman, and between your seed (offspring) and her Seed; He shall **[fatally] bruise/crush your head,** and you shall **[only] bruise** His heel" (Genesis 3:15 AMP, also see Romans 16:20).

NON-VENOMOUS & DISARMED

Finally, "non-venomous" can also point to the fact that God disarmed the venom of the snake, which bit Paul on the island of Malta (Acts 28:1-5). Just like He took the heat from the fire, for Daniel's three companions in Babylon (Daniel 3:27) and furthermore (supernaturally) shut the mouths of lions for Daniel; intercepting both sharp teeth and keen appetites! (Daniel 6:22)

As we know, our foe is already dethroned, disarmed and defeated (Colossians 2:14-15). But he still acts like he has an abundance of venom, ferocious heat; razor-sharp teeth and an unquenchable appetite. It's our responsibility to remind him who and what *he* is now. Even better, remind him who and what *we* are — in Christ — including what we now own!

In this book we have dissected Acts chapter 16 and the questions concerning python are many. Chiefly, why is divination likened to a python? Is it because the spirit python really acts like a python does in its own natural habitat? Are we to believe that a spirit of divination really suffocates and strangles or is this just metaphorical?

WITCHCRAFT IS BIBLICALLY FORBIDDEN:

While Acts 16 is the only place in the bible where the "spirit of python" is explicitly mentioned and isn't repeated elsewhere, the bible frequently warns against divination, sorcery, and false spiritual practices, for example Deuteronomy 18:10-12 and Isaiah 8:19.

> There shall not be found among you anyone who makes his son or daughter pass through the fire [as a sacrifice], one who uses *divination and fortune-telling, one who practices witchcraft, or one who interprets omens, or a sorcerer, or one who casts a charm or spell, or a medium, or a spiritist, or a necromancer [who seeks the dead].*

> ...For these nations which you shall dispossess *listen to those who practice witchcraft and to diviners and fortune-tellers,* but as for you, the LORD your God has *not allowed you to do so.*
>
> Deuteronomy 18:10-14 AMP

> When the people [instead of trusting God] say to you, *"Consult the mediums [who try to talk to the dead] and the soothsayers who chirp and whisper and mutter,"* should not a people consult their God? *Should they consult the dead on behalf of the living?* [Direct those people] to the law and to the testimony!

> *...They [who consult mediums and soothsayers] will pass through the land deeply distressed and hungry, and when they are hungry,* they will become enraged and will curse their king and their God as they look upward. Then they will look to the earth, they will see only distress and darkness, the gloom

of anguish; and *they will be driven away into darkness and overwhelming night.*

Isaiah 8:19-22 AMP

PYTHON'S INFLUENCE IN THE REGION: (FALSE PROPHECY)

Even today, when apostles go into regions, they must discern the spiritual climate. For example Paul would have understood the pagan influences and the prevailing thinking at that particular time and place. He knew what he was up against. The servant girl was not an isolated incident or a random insignificant occurrence. This demon spirit manifested an open threat because it was marking its territory.

Paul knew that he had come to do gospel business—in a hostile environment and not drink tea and biscuits with the local gentry! By challenging their belief system and entire way of life, also meant challenging their economy! So, the spread of Christianity posed a significant threat to the ancient pagan world.

Paul would have known the significance of false prophecy tied to *pythōn,* the Greek mythological serpent that guarded Delphi (home to the famous Oracle of Apollo). AND the enormous influence it had on the populace there and how they would respond to hearing the good news of the gospel for the first time.

So let's take a brief look at the region Paul landed in— and was led directly to—by the Holy Spirit.

THE SIGNIFICANCE OF THE REGION

Why Greece? Why not somewhere else in Europe? Why did the Holy Spirit specifically choose Greece as the first spiritual GATEWAY for spreading the gospel to the rest of Europe?

THE IMPORTANCE OF LANGUAGES:

One obvious and widely accepted answer is the language. Greek and Latin was widely used at that time, making the spread of the gospel faster — but not necessarily easier — for those propagating it! But it certainly helped carry the gospel more rapidly across the Greco-Roman world.

THE SIGNIFICANCE OF KOINE GREEK:
(LINGUA FRANCA)

Koine (meaning "common") was a simplified and widely spoken common dialect, making it accessible to everyday people across diverse regions (unlike the classical Greek of philosophers like Plato or Aristotle!) *Koine* emerged after Alexander the Great's conquests and became the universal language for trade, education, and culture. So at this particular time, a linguistic unity had emerged, which allowed the gospel message to cross cultural and geographic boundaries quickly.

The fact that the New Testament was written in *Koine Greek*, shows the preciseness and exactitude of the Holy Spirit's strategic genius! Being the common language of the eastern Mediterranean during the time of the Roman Empire meant that the gospel message was accessible to the majority of the people right across the empire. This was a significantly broad audience!

This also means that significant gaps between different cultures were bridged and made the scriptures understandable to Jews and Gentiles alike. Paul's letters for instance could be read and understood by early Christian communities and enjoy a wide circulation. No other time in history offered such versatility — reflecting the divine providence of perfect timing — in a highly interconnected world.

THE SIGNIFICANCE OF LATIN: (LESS DOMINANT)

Even though Latin was the official language of the Roman Empire, (especially in the western regions), Greek remained dominant in the eastern Mediterranean, including Greece, Asia Minor, Egypt, and parts of the Middle East. This made Greek the primary language of communication in many cities ensuring that the good news would be understood by a very diverse audience.

For this reason, it's abundantly clear why the gospel was brought to Europe, starting in Greece. It was above all a very prominent spiritual GATEWAY at a very precise juncture in history having a profound impact on the expansion of Christianity.

AN INTELLECTUAL HUB: (SPREAD OF IDEAS)

Greece, with its philosophical traditions and bustling trade cities, was also a cultural and intellectual hub. By traveling to and preaching in cities like Philippi, Thessalonica, Athens, and Corinth and Ephesus, Paul reached influential urban centres where ideas could spread quickly, through established trade routes (commerce) and major communication networks.

THE BENEFITS OF ROMAN INFRASTRUCTURE: (SPEED)

Additionally, the benefits of Roman infrastructure (such as roads and safe sea routes), provided stability and speed. Making travel easier and safer, further facilitated the spread of the gospel. So once again, the combination of a shared language, interconnected cities, and the Roman Empire's sturdiness, created the perfect environment for the rapid growth of Christianity.

THE SIGNIFICANCE OF DELPHI:

Delphi was one of the most significant religious centres in ancient Greece. People traveled from all over the Mediterranean to consult the "Oracle," seeking guidance on everything from personal decisions to state affairs. The priestess, known as the Pythia, would enter a trance-like state and speak prophecies that priests would interpret for those seeking answers.

Long before the emergence of Christianity (which brought the gospel/good news on the scene), the Oracle of Apollo at Delphi had a profound influence on ancient Greek—and even wider Mediterranean—history. People believed that the Pythia, channeled the voice of Apollo, (giving divine guidance). The process of consultation was a significant ritual, and many ancient figures, including kings and generals, came to Delphi to seek Apollo's counsel.

CONSULTING THE ORACLE:

The Oracle played a significant role in shaping the religious and political landscape of the time. It's influence was *immense,* as decisions ranging from military campaigns to personal matters were often guided by her words. The Greek city-states also believed that consulting the Oracle was a way to maintain their relationship with the gods, ensuring divine favour in their affairs.

Interestingly, the Oracle's influence wasn't limited to just Greece. It extended across the Mediterranean world, with people from as far as Egypt and Persia making pilgrimages to Delphi for guidance. This made Delphi a hub of religious and political power, not just a local Greek site.

THE RISE OF CHRISTIANITY:

The Oracle's decline came with the rise of Christianity. In the fourth century, Roman Emperor Theodosius I ordered the closure of pagan temples, and Delphi was abandoned. By this time, the Oracle's power had already waned as Christianity spread throughout the Roman Empire.

This better explains why their reaction was so strong when they bitterly announced before the Roman magistrates, **"They're pushing their Jewish religion down our throats. It's wrong and unlawful for them to promote these Jewish ways, for we are Romans living in a Roman colony"** (Acts 16:21 TPT).

THE CITY OF PHILIPPI: (SPIRITUALLY CHARGED)

In Acts 16, the spirit possessing the slave girl is called a "spirit of Python" (or divination) because it reflects this cultural understanding of supernatural or deceptive prophetic power. However, Paul, through the Holy Spirit, demonstrates the authority of Christ by casting out the spirit, challenging not only its power but also the cultural systems *profiting* from such practices.

When Paul traveled to places like Philippi, he was encountering a deeply ingrained spiritual atmosphere, shaped by ancient beliefs and practices (like those of Delphi). These cities were spiritually charged environments because it was long baked-in!

Philippi, with its Roman influence and Greek culture, the people were used to seeking guidance from spiritual sources. This made it a challenging and competitive environment for Paul and other early Christians who preached the gospel of Christ, which offered a very different kind of spiritual authority.

The "spirit of python" in Acts 16 reflects this environment — where supernatural, deceptive powers were at work, offering false or distorted spiritual guidance. When Paul cast out the spirit of divination, he wasn't just confronting an individual but challenging the broader spiritual system that people were relying on for truth and direction.

This offers more insight into the kind of spiritual battle Paul faced in the ancient world and vividly showcases the power of the gospel in breaking through even the most entrenched spiritual strongholds.

SPIRITUAL GATEWAYS OF THE REGION

FINAL RECAP:

In the context of Acts 16 and the spread of the gospel, here's how Macedonia, Philippi, and Delphi connect in order of significance as spiritual gateways that Paul the apostle and his team encountered:

1. Macedonia:

This is the broader region that Paul was specifically called to in his vision of the "man of Macedonia" (Acts 16:9-10). Macedonia holds the greatest significance in the passage because Paul's journey there marked the first recorded entry of the gospel into Europe. It was a pivotal moment in Christian history, as the region served as a GATEWAY for spreading Christianity westward.

2. Philippi:

Within Macedonia, Philippi was a key city where Paul and his companions first preached the gospel. As a Roman colony, it was strategically important and culturally influential. Philippi was where Paul encountered Lydia (the first European convert) and cast out the spirit of divination from the slave girl, leading to his imprisonment and the dramatic conversion of the jailer. The events in Philippi set the tone for the gospel's expansion in Macedonia and Europe.

3. Delphi:

While Delphi is not mentioned in Acts 16, its cultural and spiritual significance underpins the context of the "spirit of Python" that Paul confronts in Philippi. Delphi, as the centre of Greek divination and the Oracle of Apollo, influenced the Greco-Roman world's views on prophecy and supernatural power. The slave girl's "spirit of divination" would have been understood in light of this cultural background. However, Delphi's role is indirect, serving more as a backdrop for understanding the spiritual atmosphere Paul encountered.

LAST SUMMARY:

Macedonia is the overarching region of importance, Philippi is the focal city of the narrative, and Delphi provides cultural and spiritual context.

❖

CHAPTER 5

Spiritual Warfare

NEVER TAKE IT PERSONALLY

What has most people puzzled about Acts chapter 16, is why it took Paul so long to respond? I would suggest to you, that the devil wants us to *react* to everything and to take *everything* personally. Paul on the other hand knew that she was just a "servant girl." There was a much greater plan afoot and Paul would have been looking past "flesh and blood," to the real enemies of the gospel.

This brings to mind the phrase "weapons of this world" in Paul's teaching found in 2 Corinthians 10:3-4, where he says, *"For though we live in the world, we do not wage war as the world does. The weapons we fight with are not the weapons of the world.* ***On the contrary, they have divine power to demolish strongholds.***" NIV

DIVINE POWER TO DEMOLISH STRONGHOLDS

This highlights the distinction between physical weapons — used for earthly battles — and spiritual weapons, which are mighty through God for demolishing strongholds.

> For although we live in the natural realm, we don't wage a military campaign employing human weapons, using manipulation to achieve our aims. Instead, ***our spiritual weapons are energised with divine power to effectively dismantle the defences behind which people hide.***
>
> ***We can demolish every deceptive fantasy that opposes God and break through every arrogant attitude that is raised up in defiance of the true knowledge of God.*** We capture, like prisoners of war, every thought and insist that it bow in obedience to the Anointed One.
>
> 2 Corinthians 10:3-5 TPT

Paul's experience on the mission field — in Philippi — would most definitely have leant itself to his teachings in his letters to the Corinthian believers.

PYTHON USED FALSE PROPHECY

What is a spiritual stronghold and how is it demolished? A spiritual stronghold by definition, is anything that keeps us in bondage and away from the knowledge of God, (impacting individuals and entire regions). Strongholds are demolished by the anointed preaching of God's word.

Python used false prophecy and divination to hold an entire region in bondage. As already discussed, it's influence was immense.

2 Corinthians 10:4-5 and Ephesians 6:12 are key scriptures in the New Testament on this topic. A spiritual stronghold is a mindset or belief system that opposes God's truth and keeps people from living in freedom (John 8:36). It uses lies, fear and sin to influence and control lives.

Paul's teachings specifically spoke of **"demolishing"** strongholds—arguments or thoughts that set themselves against the knowledge of God. Essentially we have the mind of Christ (1 Corinthians 2:16) and all the time we have the thoughts, feelings and purposes of his mind, we are free. (Essentially, all demonic strongholds seek to create barriers between us and God's will).

False prophecy and divination—Acts 16—were used to gain a spiritual foothold. Such "forces of wickedness" can only be demolished by God's Spirit and the word of His power (Hebrews 4:12).

THE POWER OF RHEMA (SPOKEN)

Hebrews 1:3 says Jesus, **"upholds all things by the word of His power."** (Greek—*rhema*—specifically refers to "the *sayings* of the Son" or "his *spoken* word"). This means that God's Word not only created the universe but also sustains and governs everything. It has the force of divine authority to demolish strongholds and bring freedom—victory—when SPOKEN and believed.

This is why the active preaching of the gospel is essential and why Paul with his missionary team had to "go" to Philippi as "sent" ones. Mental-assent is insufficient. Divine spiritual power must be *released* into the atmosphere as we preach divinely revealed truth (Ephesians 3:10).

The gospel grows legs! Once spoken the gospel will go forth under its own power. "I am not ashamed of the gospel, **for it is the power of God** (Romans 1:16 AMP).

So, when Paul talks of dark spiritual "forces" of wickedness; the Holy Spirit is also a spiritual "force" of righteousness (but they are NOT equal opposites).

Paul had to bring the message of Jesus Christ—His death, resurrection, and offer of eternal life—to the region of Macedonia so that its transformative power could be released to liberate lives in a region dominated by the spirit of python. False prophecy and divination were replaced by the good news.

Obviously Acts 16's confrontation with the spirit of python was not limited to a slave girl; it was a ruling spirit that controlled an entire region and beyond. It wilfully tried to prevent the apostolic mission before it got started.

A SUCCESSFULLY DISMANTLED STRONGHOLD:

"Demolish" is another word for "dismantle." And secular history proves that Python's stronghold was indeed dismantled, in that region. It was a process that also had a very practical out-working. For instance, in the previous chapter I mentioned that paganism waned as a result of Christianity spreading throughout the Roman Empire.

To expand on this; it is well documented in historical journals that Emperor Theodosius I, played a significant role in the **closure of pagan temples,** including the Temple of Apollo at Delphi.

In the late fourth century AD, he issued decrees **outlawing pagan practices and ordered the closure of temples as part of efforts to establish Christianity as the dominant religion of the Roman Empire.**

Delphi, (which had already declined in prominence), was abandoned as a religious centre after this decree. Pagan rituals at the site ceased, and **the area transitioned to Christian use over time, with the temple eventually falling into ruin due to neglect** (and later natural disasters like earthquakes), which marked the definitive end of Delphi's role as a major spiritual and cultural hub.

In short, God used Theodosius to outlaw paganism (which meant the end of python) which was a pivotal moment in history that transitioned the entire Roman Empire away from religious pluralism — to a new state religion and a predominantly Christian society!

SO THIS, is what it looks like when a stronghold has been dismantled. Resulting in REAL, LASTING AND SUSTAINABLE CHANGE, ON A HUGE SCALE.

BREAKTHROUGHS & POWER ENCOUNTERS:

Clearly, our spiritual weapons "are mighty through God" and operate by prayer, faith and the power of the Holy Spirit. When Paul and Silas were imprisoned, their prayers and high-praises lead to a supernatural earthquake, "that shook the foundations of the prison" and "...*all* the doors were opened and *everyone's* bands were loosed" (Acts 16:26 KJV).

This was a direct result of "prayer and praise," which are spiritual weapons, not reliant on human force, but the divine. And they work!

SELF-PRESERVATION VS. THE WILL OF GOD:

We must take battles where they belong; to the realm of the spirit. And we don't take such battles personally (none of us are immune to doing this occasionally, especially when we are tired).

It's hard sometimes because the devil uses people. BUT our spiritual "struggle" is never against *people*. "Our struggle is **not against flesh and blood,** but against the rulers, against the authorities, against the powers of this dark world and against the spiritual forces of evil in the heavenly realms" (Ephesians 6:12 NIV; John 17:14-16 KJV).

Once we start taking things personally, we fall into self-preservation mode, which makes us lose our focus and purpose (Christ's agenda was never self-preservational). This pulls us out of the will of God. We become defensive, weak and our sensitivity to God (discernment) becomes seriously impaired.

All spiritual warfare is targeted at Christ (hence antichrist); therefore not personal. Remembering this prevents the root of bitterness, (Hebrews 12:15).

SO WHY THE DELAYED RESPONSE, PAUL?

We know that Paul's mission was entirely directed by divine guidance, **"...They were forbidden by the Holy Spirit to preach the word in Asia"** (Right place — wrong time). Paul's team were quick to respond to the Holy Spirit's discernible prompting, "Now after he (Paul) had seen the vision, *immediately* we sought to go to Macedonia, **concluding that the Lord had called us to preach the gospel to them"** (see Acts 16:6-11 NKJV).

So why the delay? Did this same Paul — who responded "immediately" — suddenly become delinquent? Did her harassment for "many days" exhaust and frustrate Paul to the point where he could not hear God? Or was it Paul's waiting on the unction of the Holy Spirit that delayed his response?

To the undiscerning mind — in the heat of the moment — Paul was slow to respond. (Similar perhaps to Jesus' scribbling in the dirt! Who staying very calm, didn't rush to act either, see John 8:1-11). Satan wants us to lose our rag.

Paul didn't necessarily stay calm, cool and collected either; we know he got "greatly annoyed and worn out" (Acts 16:18 AMP). Hot under the collar perhaps. But he kept his act together and ignored her for "several days." (The King James says, "many days"). The Holy Spirit will cause us to be patient too. And we must follow His lead, if we want the same results.

It takes great discernment to distinguish what's really happening, at times. On a purely human level, we've all been "annoyed and worn out" (especially in the ministry!)

Even if Paul was frustrated and spiritually exhausted, it was to his credit that he didn't ACT on it, (unlike Moses who actually did strike the rock). Remembering that the slave girl was successfully set free of demonic possession (not just oppression), and the jailer's entire household received the gospel, believe and were baptised. Then ultimately, the spirit of python dominating that region was ousted and the gospel went forth with power. I'd say Paul was effective. (Human? Yes. Delinquent? No).

THE REST IS HISTORY

The people who [are spiritually mature and] know their God will display strength and take action [to resist].

Daniel 11:32 AMP

We must keep our eyes on what's above and not what's beneath, "Yes, feast on all the treasures of the heavenly realm and fill your thoughts with heavenly realities, and not with the distractions of the natural realm" (Colossians 3:2; Psalm 121:1-2 TPT).

Many other miracles surrounded these events. The key being that Paul was obedient and did not run from spiritual warfare. Being knowledgable of the scriptures, he could no doubt recognise the diabolical ploy to "ware them out" and make them ineffective. But it failed and the rest was history.

❖

CHAPTER 6

False Prophecy

DEFINING WHAT MAKES A FALSE PROPHET

As we have seen, false prophecy was a major component of the python spirit's activity. Therefore it is important to very clearly define what makes a false prophet and what makes a true prophet, going by the biblical standard alone.

For example, in the New Testament, we know there are those who go about in sheep's clothing but are wolves. Who preach an entirely different gospel.

The theme of this book is the spirit of python, which specialised in false prophecy, which it used to hold a tremendous influence on an entire region of the ancient world.

We must be on our guard, because just as the apostolic ministry has been restored, so has paganism and false prophecy, which are operating in full force today. But just as it did then, and still true today; it takes the apostolic ministry to deal with them correctly.

FALSE PROPHETS

Biblically, false prophets are often described as deceivers who lead people away from God's truth, promoting doctrines or behaviours contrary to His will. A false prophet is someone who claims to speak on behalf of God (or possess divine insight) but misleads others through false teachings, predictions, or actions. They might use charisma or partial truths to gain followers but ultimately lack alignment to God — His Word and His Spirit (Matthew 7:15-20; 2 Peter 2:1).

Jesus said,

> *Beware of the false prophets, [teachers] who come to you dressed as sheep [appearing gentle and innocent], but inwardly are ravenous wolves. By their fruit you will recognise them [that is, by their contrived doctrine and self-focus].*
>
> Do people pick grapes from thorn bushes or figs from thistles? Even so, every healthy tree bears good fruit, but the unhealthy tree bears bad fruit. A good tree cannot bear bad fruit, nor can a bad tree bear good fruit. Every tree that does not bear good fruit is cut down and thrown into the fire. *Therefore, by their fruit you will recognise them [as false prophets].*
>
> Not everyone who says to Me, "Lord, Lord," will enter the kingdom of heaven, but only he who does the will of My Father

who is in heaven. Many will say to Me on that day [when I judge them], "Lord, Lord, have we not prophesied in Your name, and driven out demons in Your name, and done many miracles in Your name?"

And then I will declare to them publicly, "I never knew you; DEPART FROM ME [you are banished from My presence], YOU WHO ACT WICKEDLY [disregarding My commands]."

Matthew 7:15-23 AMP

KEY SCRIPTURAL WARNINGS: (FALSE PROPHETS)

False prophets lead people away from God, cultivating spiritual recklessness and moral decay. Although there are many, here are just a few key warnings concerning false prophets in the bible.

WARNINGS FROM JESUS:

As quoted at length above, Matthew 7:15-20, Jesus warns to "beware of false prophets, who come to you in sheep's clothing but inwardly are ravenous wolves." He explains that we will know them by their fruits — what they produce in their own lives and inspire in others.

OLD TESTAMENT WARNINGS:

In Jeremiah 23:16, God warns against listening to false prophets, "Do not listen to the words of the [false] prophets who prophesy to you. They are teaching you worthless things and are leading you into futility; They speak a vision of their own mind and imagination and not [truth] from the mouth of the LORD" (AMP). Such prophets told people what they wanted to hear rather than calling them to repentance.

"Hear this, I am against those who have prophesied false and made-up dreams," says the LORD, "and have told them and have made My people err and go astray by their lies and by their reckless boasting; yet *I did not send them or command them nor do they benefit and enhance [the life of] these people in the slightest way,"* says the LORD.

Jeremiah 23:32 AMP

Oh yes, I've had it with the prophets who preach the lies they dream up, spreading them all over the country, ruining the lives of my people with their cheap and reckless lies. "I never sent these prophets, never authorised a single one of them. They do nothing for this people—nothing!" MSG

NEW TESTAMENT WARNINGS:

Peter warns that false prophets will exploit people and lead them astray for personal gain:

In the past there arose false prophets among God's people, just as there will continue to be false teachers who will secretly infiltrate in your midst to divide you, bringing with them their destructive heresies... bringing swift destruction on themselves... *they are prophets who love profit...* They are following the example of Balaam, son of Beor, who was rebuked for evil by a donkey... and restrained the prophet's madness.

2 Peter 2:1,15-16 TPT

SIGNS AND WONDERS:

The focus is on whether their message aligns with God's truth. In Deuteronomy 13:1-3, God warns that even if a prophet performs signs or wonders yet encourages the worship of other gods, they are false.

CHARACTERISTICS OF FALSE PROPHETS:

They distort God's Word for personal gain (Micah 3:11). They prophesy peace when there isn't any (Ezekiel 13:10). Seek to deceive even God's elect (Matthew 24:24).

THE ROAD TO BECOMING A FALSE PROPHET

LACK OF ACCOUNTABILITY: (REBELLIOUS SPIRIT)

To finish this discussion about what defines a false prophet; ultimately a false prophet has a lack of accountability. All ministries, even apostles, must be team players and must work in relationship to the rest of the body (with apostolic connections).

There must be someone who is your oversight. Someone you LISTEN to. Someone you can submit yourself to. Otherwise you become a lone-ranger or witchy. There's no room in the body of Christ for weird isolationists or disembodiments!

There are many young ministry gifts (young apostles) who think that they can submit to the Holy Spirit alone, and don't understand that the connections God used to ordain them, were there for a reason.

Another word to the wise, "Don't be fearful of control, because that's the road to becoming a false prophet." In other words, if your excuse for becoming a loose-cannon and a dangerous liability is because you fear being controlled, then you're a fool — scripturally speaking! (See Proverbs 12:15; 13:20; 15:5; 18:2)

Remember a right spirit is always submitted. It is not independent to the rest of the body (not a free radical or a cancerous cell), and a right spirit always has the power of God behind it. There's no rebellion in Christ.

TRUE PROPHETS

A true prophet is someone chosen and inspired by God to deliver His message (rhema), often calling people to repentance, guiding them in truth, or revealing God's plans. So biblically, true prophets are those who do the following:

1. Speak in Alignment with God's Word:

Again, in Deuteronomy 13:1-5, God emphasises that even if a prophet performs miracles, their teachings must align with worshipping the one true God. A true prophet's message will never contradict scripture.

2. Their Predictions Originate from God:
(Not Imagination)

True prophets deliver messages that are reliable and accurate because they originate from God. In Deuteronomy 18:21-22, God explains that if a prophet's predictions fail to come true, they are not speaking from Him.

3. They Focus on God's Glory: (Not their Own)

They humbly carry out their mission, often enduring persecution for speaking hard truths (Jeremiah 1:9-10; John 7:18). True prophets point people to God, not themselves.

4. Exemplify Godly Character: (Fruits)

Again, their *fruits* give them away, (the results of their own behaviour and obedience — or lack thereof). Their fruits reflect the type of connection to God they have if any (Matthew 7:16-20). A true prophet lives a life consistent with their message, displaying godliness, humility, and integrity .

5. Bring People Closer to God: (Fulness)

True prophets such as Isaiah, Jeremiah, Elijah, challenged sin and called people back to a full relationship with God — often acting as His voice — during times of spiritual decline.

Examples of true prophets in the bible also include: **Moses**, (who led the Israelites and revealed God's law); **Samuel**, (who guided Israel faithfully); and **John the Baptist**, (who prepared the way for Jesus).

ONLY TRANSFORMED LIVES INHERIT THE KINGDOM OF GOD

The overarching theme here is repentance, faith in Jesus, and a transformed life through the Holy Spirit. And in 1 Corinthians 6:9-10, Paul lists behaviours that prevent people from inheriting the kingdom of God, such as sexual immorality, idolatry, theft, greed, drunkenness, and more.

Similarly, Galatians 5:19-21 speaks about the "works of the flesh" and warns that those who practice such things will not inherit God's kingdom.

On the other hand, passages like Matthew 5:3-12 (the Beatitudes) describe the kind of attitudes and actions — like humility, mercy, purity, and peacemaking — that are blessed and aligned with inheriting the kingdom of God.

PROPHECY OPERATES BY
REVEALED KNOWLEDGE

Prophecy comes from a place of *revelation;* either demonic or divine (revelation genuinely received by the Holy Spirit). Paul, when referring to his famous encounter with Jesus on the road to Damascus, said of revelation knowledge, "So you see, King Agrippa, I have not been disobedient to what was *revealed to me from heaven*" (Acts 26:19 TPT).

True rhema transforms our lives. After a genuine encounter with revealed truth, we can never be the same. Just like you can't un-ring a bell or get toothpaste back in a tube, or un-say words spoken for example. Once real change occurs — as a result of rhema — it's forever.

We can only base our lives on and be obedient to what has been *revealed* to us from heaven. Only then can we preach that to others. Divinely imparted or downloaded truth.

> For it was in Damascus that I first declared the truth. And then I went to Jerusalem and throughout our nation, and even to other nations, telling people everywhere that they must repent and turn to God and *demonstrate it with a CHANGED LIFE.*
>
> Acts 26:20 TPT

TRUTH IS OUR PLUMB-LINE

The following is an easy plumb-line test for determining whether prophecy is true or false. Ask yourself the following questions.

DOES THIS REVELATION OR PROPHECY:

- Align with scripture?

- Reinforce God's word in my life?

- Lead me closer to Christ's Person?

- Inspire me to love His body world wide?

- Strengthen & encourage my personal faith?

- Promote a lifestyle of sanctification & holiness?

- Or promote a lifestyle of narcissism?

- Discourage sin and wrongdoing in my life?

- Corroborate with other trusted bible teachers?

- Build up & edify the church?

- Train & equip saints for works of service?

SPIRITUAL CONTRABAND

To close out this chapter, let me say that we have a responsibility to recognise when someone is trafficking in spiritual contraband (especially false prophecy/charismatic witchcraft!)

> Do not quench [subdue, or be unresponsive to the working and guidance of] the [Holy] Spirit. **Do not scorn or reject gifts of prophecy or prophecies [spoken revelations—words of instruction or exhortation or warning].** But **test all things carefully [so you can recognise what is good]. Hold firmly to that which is good.**
>
> 1 Thessalonians 5:19-21 AMP

Let two or three prophets speak [as inspired by the Holy Spirit], while the rest pay attention and weigh carefully what is said... for the spirits of prophets are subject to the prophets [the prophecy is under the speaker's control, and he can stop speaking]; for God [who is the source of their prophesying] is not a God of confusion and disorder but of peace and order.

1 Corinthians 14:29-33 AMP

Beloved, do not believe every spirit [speaking through a self-proclaimed prophet]; instead test the spirits to see whether they are from God, because many false prophets and teachers have gone out into the world. By this you know and *recognise the Spirit of God:* every spirit that acknowledges and confesses [the fact] that Jesus Christ has [actually] come in the flesh [as a man] *is from God [God is its source].*

1 John 4:1-2 AMP

DISCERN THE SOURCE:

Just like Paul did with the servant girl of Acts 16. He discerned that she had a wrong spirit, even though the right words were coming out of her mouth. She was mocking and goading them. The source was not God.

Remember Satan is the lawless one. Jesus is the righteous one. What He speaks is SPIRIT and LIFE.

The Holy Spirit is the one who gives life, that which is of the natural realm is of no help. *The words I speak to you are Spirit and life.*

John 6:63 TPT

❖

CHAPTER 7

Spiritual Weariness & Exhaustion

NOT AGE RELATED

As we were on our way **to the place of prayer,** we were met by a slave girl who was possessed by a spirit of divination... Then Paul, being **sorely annoyed and <u>worn out,</u>** turned and said to the spirit within her, I charge you in the name of Jesus Christ to come out of her! (Acts 16:16-18 AMPC)

> He shall speak great words against the most High, and shall **WEAR OUT THE SAINTS OF THE MOST HIGH,** and think to change times and laws: and they shall be given into his hand until a time and times and the dividing of time.
>
> Daniel 7:25 KJV

The devil always wants to divert us from praying. Evidently this did not stop Paul and his crew. But no matter how long we've been doing this, or how mature we become, sometimes all the spiritual noise and manifestations become so deafening and sustained that weariness creeps in.

Nonetheless Isaiah comforts us by saying, **"Even <u>youths</u> shall faint and be weary,** and [selected] **young men shall feebly stumble** *and* <u>**fall exhausted"**</u> (Isaiah 40:30 AMPC). Evidently then, spiritual weariness is not an age related phenomena. Exhaustion is not always physical, it's very often spiritual (or combined).

Something that comes on us like a thick cloak, that oppresses us, our minds and our bodies. In fact I'd say that many people are spiritually exhausted and don't even know it. They feel bad about themselves, when all they need to do, is take authority and get out from under it. (In Christ we are above, not beneath, see Ephesians 2:6).

EVEN YOUNG MEN IN THEIR PRIME:

Young men in their prime can feel like old men, when spiritual weariness comes upon them. I knew of a young pastor in his late-twenties, who went through a very painful divorce. The surrounding circumstances were very brutal. Yet being a very sincere young man, didn't pursue divorce from his wife (who had been unfaithful to him). He tried at length to salvage his marriage, but to no avail.

During this time, (with very young children in toe) this man found it hard just getting out of bed in the morning. His body ached all over like an old man's, just from stress. And only after receiving a timely word from his spiritual father (a word of wisdom that profoundly revived him), did he begin to recover. His body felt young again, all the aches and pains went away. I'm telling you folks... *this is spiritual.*

I can also affirm, that this kind of experience has happened to me, on more than one occasion. It comes on you so subtly, that you don't even notice, at first. You assume its just age related. In fact when you're so distracted by the trouble you're in, you take no thought for yourself, until you can barely stand.

WHEN SLEEP OFFERS NO RELIEF:

You feel more tired in the morning, than when you went to bed. Once you finally realise you're under attack, you are already "greatly annoyed and worn out." (As ministers we're so busy "doing ministry" that we forget to minister to ourselves).

Can you relate with this? Have you ever experienced something like this? You'll know it's not merely physical, when after you pray, the exhaustion leaves as quickly as it came. (That's when you know it was totally spiritual).

Many people have told me their experiences, so I know this is not rare. Stress and unresolved trauma can wreak havoc and have been linked to illnesses such as fibromyalgia, (but this is for another conversation). Sadly, **unresolved trauma causes needless suffering.**

However in the book of Galatians 6:9 it warns, "Let us not become weary..." (NIV). In other translations it reads,

"Let us not grow weary or become discouraged in doing good, for at the proper time we will reap, if we do not give in" (AMP). "Let's not allow ourselves to get fatigued... give up, or quit" (MSG).

WEARINESS DEFINED:

The Greek definition for weariness means, **"To be utterly spiritless, to be wearied out, exhausted"** (Strong's G1573). (Exhaustion comes from the Latin word *exhaurire "drain out"*). The english definition for weary is, "lacking strength, energy, or freshness because of a need for rest or sleep; **annoyed** by something... done many times ('many days') or for a long time; causing you to feel tired" (Merriam-Webster).

"Utterly spiritless and exhausted," adequately describes the young pastor who was suffering emotional and physical exhaustion. But it was a spiritual attack on his life and ministry.

Worn-out-saints, pose no threat. All the time we remain full of vigour and strength on the other hand, we pose a very real threat to the enemy. But how do we achieve this? Isaiah tells us how, in chapter 40:31, "They that **wait upon the Lord** shall renew their strength; they shall... not be weary... and not faint" (KJV).

WAITING ON THE LORD RENEWS STRENGTH

Waiting on the Lord has the ability to "renew our strength" which in turn helps us avoid "weariness." This is a common sense matter to me. We must learn the art of "waiting." And according to the original language (Hebrew) waiting means, to look for, hope for, to expect, to look eagerly for, to lie in wait for, to linger for, to be collect/ed and bound together (Strong's H6960).

For me, these definitions could preach by themselves. And I could preach an hour on each one but space won't allow. The ones that stand out are, **"lying in wait"** and **"lingering for."** I like also the idea of being **"bound together"** with the Lord through the process of "lingering." Being "collected" talks of composure. Paul displayed composure—even though greatly annoyed—was not rash.

All in all, waiting on the Lord, does not give us the picture of erratic behaviour. (Many years of ministry have taught me the lessons of acting rashly!) People, who wait patiently for God's instruction, are never the types who live from one knee-jerk-reaction to another.

In fact people who are mature in the things of the Spirit, who have learnt to be led (under years of pressure) by the Holy Spirit, are some of the most composed people you'll ever meet.

JESUS HAD THE COOL FACTOR!

No one has ever displayed as much *cool-factor* as Jesus. "They got up, drove him out of the town, and took him to the brow of the hill on which the town was built, in order to throw him off the cliff. **But he walked right through the crowd and went on his way.** Then he went down to Capernaum ...he taught the people" (Luke 4:29-31 NIV). Unmoved and undeterred Jesus went on his way, with a business as usual attitude, to teach the people, (very smooth).

Going back to Paul being tormented for, "many days" (KJV). Imagine, just a few hours of something drains us, but days?! And it's for this reason the devil is persistent. He knows it's just a matter of time. No matter how spiritually mature we are. And hearing how "annoyed and worn out" Paul was, makes us realise just how normal we really are. If he struggled to stay composed, how much more will we be tested?

Too much attention given to the wrong things — at the wrong time — makes them worse. We must rely on the Holy Spirit, (we've got no business provoking or chasing devils). God chose to bless us in the presence of our enemies, meaning that they get to see how blessed we are! The idea is that we're fixated on God, no one else.

> Thou preparest a table before me *in the presence of mine enemies:* thou anointest my head with oil; my cup runneth over.
> Psalm 23:5 KJV

> You serve me a six- course dinner *right in front of my enemies.* You revive my drooping head; my cup brims with blessing. MSG

IGNORING PYTHON: (FIXATE ON GOD IN PRAYER)

Jesus never asked for his disciples to be rescued but protected; there's a difference. "I pray not that thou shouldest take them out of the world, but that thou shouldest keep them from the evil" (John 17:15 KJV). Some people are so fixated on the wrong things, they actually end up talking to devils more than they talk to God.

Paul openly ignored this python spirit, until he didn't. Meaning he didn't give it more oxygen than was necessary.

Until the Holy Spirit instructed him to act; maybe for a wider audience to assemble!

"When the enemy shall come in like a flood, the Spirit of the Lord shall lift up a standard against him" (Isaiah 59:19 KJV). Likewise, when the tide comes in, all the boats rise. Perhaps the Holy Spirit had this in mind — orchestrating events — to reveal gospel to as many as possible.

Notice, that although deliverance is the children's bread — and the slave girl was not a believer — Paul cast the spirit out in the name of Jesus regardless, which demonstrated that deliverance can also extend to non-believers, showcasing God's power and mercy.

THE KEY: KNOWING WHEN TO ACT & WHEN NOT TO

Striking the balance between knowing when to act and when to ignore, is important. "You will guard him *and* keep him in perfect and constant peace whose mind... is STAYED ON YOU" (Isaiah 26:3 AMPC).

Finally, notice how we never see Paul repenting for being, "annoyed and worn out." But we do know that the spirit of divination (python) was out to destroy Paul and discredit his apostolic company. We can learn a lot from this. To guard ourselves from weariness otherwise tormenting spirits have a much easier time of harassing and steering us away from God's presence; when we are tired and at our whits' end.

While the devil can't "stop" the apostolic ministry, he'll use all measure of delay tactics and mockery to discredit and distract instead. So we must stay fresh, in the anointing. Communing with God intimately — relationship not formula — daily. It's our most effective safeguard.

❖

CHAPTER 8

Narcism

TODAY'S CULTURE OF EXTREME SELFISHNESS

Extreme **Narcism,** is linked to divination and the python spirit because it is intertwined. We know that chapter 16 of the book of Acts tells us how the servant girl who was "possessed" by the python spirit, "... brought her owners much gain by her fortunetelling" (Acts 16:16).

FINANCES GET HIT

The repercussions of this incident were huge, because at the very heart of it, money was involved. Verse 19 in the Voice Translation says, "...her owners realised she would be **worthless** now as a fortune-teller." And the Message Bible says, **"When her owners saw that their lucrative little**

business was suddenly bankrupt, they went after Paul and Silas, roughed them up..."

This spirit not only wants to divert our attention from prayer, it also wants to **divert our funds,** from fulfilling God's plans. When you live by faith, as I have for many years, you'll discover, that when the unity goes, so will your income! Living by faith means you can't live in the flesh. You don't get away with it. So you have to keep the unity at all costs, otherwise the devil gets in.

As much as divination and the spirit of python want to annoy and wear us out, it wants to influence our income. If it can bankrupt us by using greed to siphon-off resources, then we become ineffective and non-productive. Ministries everywhere including Christian businesses—dedicated to the work of God—can suddenly start haemorrhaging money.

Usually mismanagement and greed are to blame, "You can be sure of this: No one will have a place in the kingdom of Christ and of God who... is greedy. **Anyone who is greedy is serving a false god"** (Ephesians 5:5 NCV). The Voice Translation says it this way, **"greed... is just a form of idolatry."**

TAKING AUTHORITY OVER YOUR FINANCES:

As we have already stated, only once Paul took authority, did he put a stop to this demon's noise. And by experience, I can tell you, that divination and the spirit of python are after your finances too. So, in the same context, if you want your finances to be free from python's influence, then you must take authority.

To divert your funds it has to get you to mismanage them, where you or your people spend money on the wrong things.

God has ordained good works for us to do. But if the money dries up, your hands are tied. You can't move left or right (and frustration sets in). For example, people who where once reliable and generous in their giving, start being more sensitive to their own needs, than the Spirit of God.

They switch allegiance and develop urgent selfish agendas. Yielding to the extreme selfishness of this culture, which is totally self-serving in nature. The spirit of this culture is narcissism and has successfully infiltrated the Church.

NARCISSISM DEFINED:

Narcissus is a fictional character from history who fell in love with himself. There are variations on this particular myth, but at it's core is SELF-WORSHIP.

Narcissus was **"a beautiful youth in Greek mythology who pined away for love of his own reflection"** (Merriam-Webster). So when someone is described as narcissistic, it refers to their self-absorbed personality traits and excessively self-centred behaviour.

Narcissistic Personality Disorder (NPD) is a disorder in which a person is *excessively preoccupied with personal adequacy* and was first recognised in 1968 but was historically seen as megalomania or severe egocentrism. "People who are diagnosed with a narcissistic personality disorder are characterised by *exaggerated feelings of self-importance.*

They have a sense of entitlement and demonstrate grandiosity in their beliefs and behaviour. They have a strong need for admiration, but lack feelings of empathy."[1]

NARCISM VS. THE FRUITS OF THE SPIRIT

I think that most people have narcissistic tendencies, in one way or another. Basically the definition above describes the fallen nature and the fruits of the flesh. Which is the opposite to divine nature and the fruits of the Spirit. Love represents the divine nature. The fallen nature is always self-serving and self-seeking.

Only as we walk by the Spirit and cultivate our love walk with the fruits of the Spirit, can we avoid this narcissistic manifestation in our own lives. **"Don't become so well-adjusted to your culture that you fit into it without even thinking... the culture around you, always dragging you down to its level of immaturity..."** (Romans 12:1-2 MSG)

In our culture today, narcissism is all around us, in the music, the arts and all other forms of entertainment. It is in the schools and education. In fact narcissism is generally celebrated and encouraged. However, as believers, scripture separates us from the culture. We are in the culture. We even reach *into* the culture. But we are not of the culture, "Do not conform to the pattern of this world..." (Romans 12:2 NIV)

"They are not of the world, even as I am not of the world" (John 17:16 KJV). Our behaviour must emulate and imitate Christ, Who revealed Himself to us as a "servant King." He came to serve and not to be served, although He was King of kings and Lord of lords. We too have position and possession (in Christ) yet **we must serve and love the people of this culture – without loving the culture.**

NARCISM & INDULGENCE

If you are looking to do anything significant for God, then be prepared for spiritual attack. Understand that your money and resources – will suffer spiritual attack – probably more than any other area.

Narcism has a great influence on today's culture (the Church is not immune) and wants people to indulge in self-love in a wrong way. So how do we recognise when narcissism has crept in? It will manifest in the people. Those who were once reliable to give and tithe are suddenly overwhelmed by their own needs and full of excuses.

Don't start complaining and becoming weary with your people. Recognise the spiritual warfare for what it is, and take the fight to the devil – not your people. "The goodness of God that leads men to repentance" (Romans 2:4 KJV). See the strangle-hold on your finances; your church, business or family and take authority over it.

IS THE DEVIL IN YOUR MIDST?

If you don't you'll become weary and frustrated. You'll start making poor decisions that will discredit you and things will get messy. **When selfishness suddenly grips all your people at once – the devil is in your midst.** Recognise him and cast him out. Keep the unity and the bond of peace, and take the battle to the enemy, not each other.

Dear friend, if you have been struggling with your finances in this season, and many have, recognise divination and the spirit of python. Cast it out of your affairs, just like Paul cast it out of the servant girl. **Leaders, you need to cast it out of your people.** This spirit has no jurisdiction — unless you permit it — so rise up and stop brooding over your losses. Stand up and proclaim liberty over yourself, your people and your finances.

Straight away, you'll begin to see change. Even if things get worse before they get better, change will happen. Speak those things that aren't as though they were and start giving God high praises (in advance) regardless of your circumstances, like Paul and Silas and take courage as chains supernaturally begin coming off. You and your people will be free again.

LEADERS GATHER YOUR PEOPLE:

Greed and selfishness scatter the people. Leaders gather your people together. Get them back into a place of unity. And bring them to a place of repentance if necessary and help them overcome individually, so that you can overcome corporately. Pray with a united front and take authority over divination and the spirit of python. And don't be intimidated by all the noise it wants to make.

Go right ahead and do what God's instructing you to do, because you have this assurance, "No weapon that can hurt you has ever been forged. Any accuser who takes you to court will be dismissed as a liar. This is what God's servants can expect. I'll see to it that everything works out for the best. God's Decree" (Isaiah 54:17 MSG).

A DRAMATIC TURN OF EVENTS

We know that divination and the spirit of python tried for many days to divert attention and create commotion. Although it did stir up a great disturbance, this just turned out to be very *superficial* in the end. We know this because in verse 38 and 39 it says, "The magistrates ...were frightened when they heard that the prisoners were Roman citizens; so they came themselves and (striving to appease them by entreaty) apologised to them. And they brought them out and asked them to leave the city."

What a dramatic turn of events. Yet you too can experience such a turn around, if you'll take your stand like Paul and Silas did. You'll go from feeling spiritually-beaten-up, to feeling normal again. And when the turbulence eventually dies down, you'll see all the awesome things God achieved in the midst of it.

God does not need a red carpet to make an entrance (He too can work in stealth). The conditions don't have to be perfect for Him to move. God will do most, when we least expect it and in the most unpredictable places. "Thou preparest a table before me in the presence of mine enemies..." (Psalm 23:5 KJV)

The lilies grow in the valley not on the mountaintop. And it's in that place of trouble that God performs life changing miracles. Paul's jailer "...brought them out [of the dungeon] and said, Men, what is it necessary for me to do that I may be saved?" (Acts 16:30 AMPC) "And they declared the word of the Lord... to him and to all who were in his house" (v32 AMPC).

God always has a purpose, beyond what the eye can see. I always tell my family and team, "When it seems like God is doing nothing, very often that's when He's doing most. Just because we can't see what's happening right now, doesn't mean that nothing's happening." So be determined to see God in every situation. He is there... moving, working-miracles and speaking to all those who have ears to hear.

❖

CHAPTER 9

Revival

A LIVING SACRIFICE

As you know, in this book I have set out to expose the nature of the spirit of python as mentioned in the book of Acts chapter 16 and the specific way it attacks and targets the apostle and the apostolic ministry, (their person, their assignment and mission, including their funds!)

> Therefore, I urge you, brothers and sisters, in view of God's mercy, to offer your bodies as a living sacrifice, holy and pleasing to God—this is your **true and proper worship.**
>
> Romans 12:1 NIV

We've seen for example, how python looks to exhaust the saints, especially the apostle, and how narcism and extreme selfishness has infiltrated the culture; even the Church to distract and make us ineffective.

The lifestyle of believers aught to be the lifestyle of a true disciple. When we experience conversion, it lasts only for a hot minute. Because the minute we choose to "follow" Christ, we step into a discipleship training program with the Holy Spirit.

Lifestyle to the true disciple of Christ is everything. Sanctification is a setting-apart for service, by and for the Holy Spirit, who goes to work on us straight away; with our cooperation of course (Matthew 28:19-20; Luke 9:23; John 13:34-35).

REVIVALS ARE NOT ABOUT SELF PROMOTION

Lifestyle is something, which I am a huge advocate for and even named our university after it, "LifeStyle International Christian University — LICU." Without lifestyle, we cannot emulate Christ. To be a witness for Christ, our words are cheap if we lack the lifestyle to back it up. We can't be hearers only but doers.

CHANGED BY HIS PRESENCE:

All those used in past revivals (including now), were emptied of themselves, first. Such individuals recognised that **revivals are not about *self promotion*,** but about what God is doing in the lives of others. The yoke destroying power is in the presence of God. Only when we remain in His presence, can our lifestyle be changed and then we'll see true revival.

When it comes to revival (especially for leadership), lifestyle is everything.

Jesus called us to a lifestyle of prayer and fasting, not narcism. When people pray and don't get results, they grow very **restless and hopeless,** because they pray with wrong motives and hidden agendas, to furnish their narcissistic desires.

FREE FROM THE GOD OF SELF:

We see this in James 4:3, "Ye ask, and receive not, because ye ask amiss, that **ye may consume it upon your lusts**" (KJV). "You do ask... and yet fail to receive, because you ask with wrong purpose and evil, selfish motives..." (AMPC) "...you know you'd be asking for what you have no right to. You're spoiled children, each wanting your own way" (MSG).

For those who have lost hope, I say to you, we will never have a future in God when we focus on ourselves. **We have to die to self.** Lust is never satisfied. But when we are full of God — lust and self — are taken care of. In Christ we lose everything, to gain everything. "Whoever wants to save their life will lose it, but whoever loses their life for me will save it" (Luke 9:24 NIV).

GODLY LIFESTYLE IS EVERYTHING:

To continue with our focus on revival, I want to look once again at the Message Bible, were it reads:

> Take your everyday, ordinary life—your sleeping, eating, going-to-work, and walking-around life—and place it before God as

an offering. Embracing what God does for you is the best thing you can do for him. Don't become so well-adjusted to your culture that you fit into it without even thinking. Instead, fix your attention on God.

You'll be changed from the inside out. Readily recognise what he wants from you, and quickly respond to it. Unlike the culture around you, always dragging you down to its level of immaturity, God brings the best out of you, develops well-formed maturity in you.

Romans 12:1 MSG

We're not here to blend our lives with the culture. We're here to live the lifestyle of God's kingdom—in front of the culture—not the other way around. Instead we must lay the dictates of this culture down, once and for all.

THE EMPHASIS IS ON LIFE & TRUST:

God is the God of the living and not the dead. In the New Testament, emphasis is now on the LIVING part of the sacrifice! A living sacrifice means trust. We are not meant to work everything out like one giant (spiritual) algorithm, but to trust God with our lives.

Usually revivals plummet, once division sets in. When division happens—get the unity back. Love stops division. Step back into God's love and lay everything down. We say that we want the anointing to destroy the yokes of bondage in our lives, but we must remain IN the anointing and not in the flesh. We must learn to move as He moves. It's a whole new lifestyle.

In his book called, Hosting the Presence, Bill Johnson writes, "I realise that we are not to live by feelings. Emotions are wonderful, but not reliable indicators of God's presence and moving. But there is a feeling that goes beyond emotions, and quite frankly can work regardless of our emotional state. It is the mood of the Holy Spirit Himself that **we can become so in tune with that we move as He moves.**"[1]

One of the greatest declarations of the bible is this, "When you draw close to God, God will draw close to you" (James 4:8 TLB) regardless whether we feel anything or not. His closeness creates a new lifestyle in us. Where we are willing to change, to meet His expectations.

SUBDUING APPETITES:

One area that God's influence in our lives helps to change is our appetite. Fasting is a conviction, (not a brooding apathy) and is a place where we learn to subdue the appetites of our flesh. **What we don't need is more information or teaching. What we need is more revelation.** Manna stank the day after. We need fresh rhema every single day.

"Give us this day our daily bread..." (Matthew 6:11 KJV), not only refers to physical food but to revelation. Even fellowship with the Holy Spirit must be daily or it will stink (metaphorically). We need to develop an appetite for fresh manna. The now word of God.

Divination and the python spirit will always draw us into idolatry and false worship (through our appetites), especially self-worship. For instance, I believe in abundance and the abundant life. I believe too in prosperity, but we were never meant to worship abundance. We must worship the one true God (of abundance), Who gives us abundant life, through Christ. We don't hoard wealth, so that we can build ourselves big golden calves to worship!

What are your appetites? Do you hunger for fame and big ministry? When I listened to Joyce Meyer recently, (and I've not listened to Joyce for a long while), I noticed that everything she said, was all about *helping others.* It was not all about making her ministry bigger or about how great the latest meetings were.

Instead after many years of ministry Joyce has learnt, that it's only as she lays big-ministry down, that God has given her a big-ministry. I only use her as an example. So many in ministry today, are actually worshipping their ministries and the size of their ministries (or churches) rather than God. What a bizarre state of affairs. Perhaps they were sincere to begin with, but somewhere along the way, agendas got swapped and they *lost the plot.*

SELF-HELP VERSUS SELF-SACRIFICE

Anyone who intends to come with me has to let me lead... **SELF-HELP is no help at all. SELF-SACRIFICE is the way,** my way...

Luke 9:23 MSG

If I had to put sound advice into one sentence, I would start by saying, **"Get into the glory and don't work it out."** Like I said above, this is not a spiritual algorithm. We'll never be able to work it all out. Instead, with supernatural words

122

of knowledge, given by God, all questions are dispelled and there's no debate. In fact when God touches our lives, all the questioning stops.

We stop questioning because we become too overwhelmed and excited with His presence. Our focus changes. We begin supernaturally trusting God to reveal what we need to know at the right time. Then we apply our lives to the right pursuits rather than exhausting ourselves by trying to be clever and working everything out by ourselves. We are not God.

People who soak up the glory all the time are beaming, happy and radiant people (to be envied!) Those who don't share the same experience on the contrary are often cynical and jealous of the experience they witness in others. They are close to the spout but they are not getting wet.

LET GOD WORK IT ALL OUT:

We must stop working it out and get into the presence of God and let Him work it out. Wherever the glory is, that's where God is speaking, "Arise, shine; for thy light is come, and the glory of the Lord is risen upon thee" (Isaiah 60:1 KJV). And we must sacrifice self-will so that we can enter His presence.

As priests of our own soul—we must sacrifice self-will every day. "Not my will but yours be done," (Luke 22:42 NIV). "Whoever wants to be my disciple must *deny themselves* and *take up their cross daily* and follow me" (Luke 9:23 NIV).

We make sacrifices on the alter of our own souls so that we can enter into God's presence. If our worship is not helping us achieve this, then it's *not* worship. "Yet a time is coming and has now come when the **true worshippers** will worship the Father in the Spirit and in truth, for **they are the kind of worshippers the Father seeks...**" (John 4:23-24 NIV)

Finally have you ever noticed how 100% tennis players are? They are ALL-IN and SOLD-OUT individuals. They are so focused, to win. We must be the same. ALL-IN BELIEVERS. But for tennis players, it's all about the tennis and not about themselves.

In fact they deny themselves many luxuries, to fulfil the demands of their sport. Equally so, it's all about Christ and not about us. If tennis players can deny themselves to follow sport, we can deny ourselves, to follow Christ.

> If any person wills to come after Me, let him *deny himself* [disown himself, forget, lose sight of himself and his own interests, refuse and give up himself] and take up his cross daily and follow Me [cleave steadfastly to Me, conform wholly to My example in living and, if need be, in dying also].
>
> For *whoever would preserve his life and save it will lose and destroy it, but whoever loses his life for My sake, he will preserve and save it* [from the penalty of eternal death].
>
> Luke 9:23-24 AMPC

❖

CHAPTER 10

Spiritual Gateways

AS DIRECTLY MENTIONED IN THE BIBLE

Gateways can represent a variety of things to different people of different cultures, (symbolically and metaphorically). But in both the physical and spiritual realms, doors and gateways always represent one major thing, "ACCESS."

Usually we are required to have authorisation or keys in order to enter anything from buildings and vehicles to technology, for example our password is our key for access (point of entry). All things require. Jesus gave us the keys of the kingdom (Matthew 16:19).

So here are a few key scriptures related to gateways/ doorways from a biblical perspective; using both the Old and New Testaments. Principally representing God's presence and access to Him—to the way of salvation—through His son Jesus Christ.

Therefore gates also signify spiritual authority, as Jesus Himself said, "I will build my church; and the **GATES OF HELL** shall not prevail against it" (Matthew 16:18 KJVS).

Then Jesus answered him, "Blessed [happy, spiritually secure, favoured by God] are you, Simon son of Jonah, because flesh and blood (mortal man) did not reveal this to you, but My Father who is in heaven. And I say to you that you are Peter, and on this rock I will build My church; and the *GATES of Hades* (death) will not overpower it [by preventing the resurrection of the Christ].

I will give you the KEYS (AUTHORITY) of the kingdom of heaven; and whatever you bind [forbid, declare to be improper and unlawful] on earth will have [already] been bound in heaven, and whatever you loose [permit, declare lawful] on earth will have [already] been loosed in heaven."

Matthew 16:17-19 AMP

OR IN THE PASSION TRANSLATION:

Jesus replied, "You are favoured and privileged Simeon, son of Jonah! For you didn't discover this on your own, but my Father in heaven has *supernaturally revealed* it to you. I give you the name Peter, a stone. And this rock will be the bedrock foundation on which *I will build my church—my legislative assembly, and the POWER OF DEATH will not be able to overpower it!* I will give you the keys of heaven's kingdom realm to forbid on earth that which is forbidden in heaven, and to release on earth that which is released in heaven."

Matthew 16:17-19 TPT

In the Passion Translation footnotes it clarifies that the Greek word for "church" is ekklesia and means "legislative assembly" or "selected ones." This is not a religious term at all, but a political and governmental term that is used many times in classical Greek for a group of people who have been summoned and **gathered together to govern the affairs of a city. For Jesus to use this term means he is giving the keys of governmental authority in His kingdom to the church.**[1]

Above, Jesus Himself directly referred to gates as spiritual authorities. And this concept of gates (in biblical times) was already baked-in to the consciousness of everyone alive at that time, because they had always symbolised power and authority.

Without the internet or a government database, city leaders would often gather at the gates; commonly seen as places of judgment and decision-making, as mentioned. Notice too that different translations of the bible use the words for gates and power, interchangeably, as emphasised above.

Authority is either legitimate or illegitimate. Which plays out throughout the bible. Jesus' authority was questioned on numerous occasions, "By what authority are you doing these things!" (See Matthew 21:23-27; Mark 11:27-33; Luke 20:1-8). Kingdom business necessitates true legal authority (see Acts 19:13-16).

His reference to "rock" can also be connected to believers as "living stones" built into a spiritual house (the church) mentioned in 1 Peter 2:5.

BIBLICAL SPIRITUAL GATEWAYS: (OLD TESTAMENT)

So many scriptures refer to gateways in the bible. One example I must mention briefly, is that of the Passover in Exodus chapter 12. I have written about this in other books, referring to the fact that if the fathers/elders of Israel had been delinquent that day, the outcome of the Passover would have been very different indeed.

Though is does not use the specific word "gateway" in Exodus, fathers are gateways to the rest of the family (this is borne out in both the Old and the New Testaments — see also Ephesians 6:1-3 and Matthew 14:21; Mark 6:44; John 6:10 for NT examples).

> Tell all the congregation of Israel, "On the tenth [day] of this month they are to take a lamb or young goat for themselves, according to [the size of] *the household of which he is the father...*
>
> Then Moses called for all the *elders of Israel* and said to them, "Go and take a lamb for yourselves *according to [the size of] your families..."*
>
> Exodus 12:3-4, 21-22 AMP

Then, with direct usage of the words gateway or portal, Jacob in the book of Genesis, awoke in "Bethel" saying, "How awesome is this place! I have stumbled right into the House of God! **THIS PLACE IS A PORTAL, THE VERY GATE OF HEAVEN!**" (Genesis 28:17 TPT) Or, "How awesome is this place! This is none other than the house of God; this is the **gate of heaven"** (Genesis 28:17 NIV). Or, **"gateway to heaven"** (AMP).

"Lift up your heads, you **gates;** be lifted up, you ancient **doors,** that the King of glory may come in" (Psalm 24:7 NIV).

> *So wake up, you LIVING GATEWAYS! Lift up your heads, you DOORWAYS OF ETERNITY!* Welcome the King of Glory, for he is about to come through you. You ask, "Who is this King of Glory?" YAHWEH, armed and ready for battle, YAHWEH, invincible in every way!
>
> *So wake up, you LIVING GATEWAYS, and rejoice! FLING WIDE, YOU ETERNAL DOORS!* Here he comes; the King of Glory is ready to come in. You ask, "Who is this King of Glory?" He is YAHWEH, armed and ready for battle, the Mighty One, the invincible commander of heaven's hosts! Yes, he is the King of Glory! Pause in his presence.
>
> Psalm 24:7-10 TPT

NEHEMIAH & THE TEN GATES OF JERUSALEM:

After the Babylonian exile, the book of Nehemiah provides a detailed account of the reconstruction of Jerusalem's walls and gates under Nehemiah's leadership. Chapter 3 lists ten gates and it could be said that each gate included in the reconstruction represents a specific stage in the believer's spiritual journey; paralleling the spiritual rebuilding that God does in their lives.

For clarity, while these ten gates are explicitly mentioned in chapter 3, other gates such as the Ephraim Gate and the

Prison Gate are noted elsewhere in the bible but are not specifically included in Nehemiah's narrative:

1. Sheep Gate: (Sacrifice & Salvation)

Located in the northeastern part of the city, this gate was used for bringing sheep into the city for temple sacrifices. Representing sacrifice and Christ as the Lamb of God, it reminds believers that their spiritual journey begins with His sacrifice.

2. Fish Gate: (Evangelism & Outreach)

Situated in the northern wall, it was named because fishermen brought their catch through this gate to the market. Therefore this gate represents spreading the Gospel and calling believers to become "fishers of men" (Matthew 4:19).

3. Old Gate: (Foundations & Truth)

Also known as the Jeshanah Gate, it was located in the northwestern section of the city and signifies the foundational unchanging truths of God (Jeremiah 6:16).

4. Valley Gate: (Humility & Dependence)

Found on the western side, it opened to the Valley of Hinnom and this gate represents trials that teach humility and reliance on God.

5. Dung Gate: (Purification & Repentance)

Located at the southern tip of the city, it was used to remove refuse and waste and so this gate symbolises humility and trials; cleansing and the removal of sin and impurities.

6. Fountain Gate: (Living Water & the Holy Spirit)

Positioned near the Pool of Siloam, it was close to the King's Garden. This gate reflects the spiritual cleansing, refreshing and life-giving work of the Holy Spirit in a believer's life.

7. Water Gate: (God's Word)

Located on the eastern side, it led to the Gihon Spring. Near this gate, Ezra read the Law to the people (Nehemiah 8:1-3), symbolising the cleansing power of God's word (Ephesians 5:26).

8. Horse Gate: (Spiritual Warfare)

Situated near the temple area, it was used by the king's horses; (associated with warfare). Therefore this gate reminds believers of the spiritual battle they face daily (Ephesians 6:12).

9. East Gate: (Christ's Return)

Facing the Mount of Olives, this gate was also called the Golden Gate; traditionally associated with the Messiah's arrival and return in glory (Ezekiel 44:1-3).

10. Inspection Gate: (Judgment & Accountability)

Also referred to as the Muster Gate, it was used for mustering troops. This gate signifies the final judgment and the believer's accountability before God.

BIBLICAL SPIRITUAL GATEWAYS: (NEW TESTAMENT)

"Enter through the narrow **gate**. For wide is the **gate** and broad is the road that leads to destruction, and many enter through it. But small is the **gate** and narrow the road that leads to life, and only a few find it" (Matthew 7:13-14 NIV).

"I AM THE GATE; whoever enters through me will be saved. They will come in and go out, and find pasture" (John 10:9 NIV).

> Jesus said to the Pharisees, "...the true Shepherd walks right up to the **gate,** and because the **gatekeeper** knows who he is, he **opens the gate** to let him in. And the sheep recognise the voice of the true Shepherd, for he calls his own by name and leads them out, for they belong to him..."

> "I speak to you eternal truth: *I am the Gate for the flock.* All those who broke in before me are thieves who came to steal, but the sheep never listened to them. *I am the Gateway.* To enter through me is to experience life, freedom, and satisfaction.
> John 10:1-3, 7-9 TPT

GATEWAY OF THE TONGUE/MOUTH

Finally in this chapter, it would be remiss of me, if I did not include the all important gateway of the tongue/mouth on which all the other gateways mentioned in this book depend.

So just briefly, let's mention a few scriptures, which reveal this truth. For example, James 3:5-6 compares the tongue to a small fire that can set a forest ablaze and Proverbs 13:3 also reveals that a big mouth, equals a big trouble!

THE KEY POINT:

The tongue/mouth brings access to life or death, destruction and ruin or eternal life. As the New Testament teaches; "**...confess with your mouth** that Jesus is Lord" (Romans 10:9 AMP).

> For if you **publicly declare with your mouth** that Jesus is Lord and believe in your heart that God raised him from the dead, you will experience salvation. The heart that believes in him receives the gift of the righteousness of God—and **then the mouth confesses, resulting in salvation.**
>
> Romans 10:9-10 TPT

> **Death and life are in the power of the tongue,** And those who love it and indulge it will eat its fruit and bear the consequences of their words.
>
> Proverbs 18:21 AMP

> He who guards his mouth preserves his life, but he who **opens wide his lips** shall have destruction.
>
> Proverbs 13:3 NKJV

Footnotes; "A person's life largely reflects the fruit of his tongue. To speak life is to speak God's perspective on any issue of life; to speak death is to declare life's negatives, to declare defeat, or complain constantly" (New Spirit- Filled Life bible).

The mouth provides access — gateway — to the kingdom of life in Christ Jesus or the kingdom of death, darkness and sin. To good or bad. Life or death. Blessing or cursing, "Out of the same mouth proceed blessing and cursing. My brethren, these things ought not to be so" (James 3:10 NKJV).

As children, we were often told, "Shut your trap!" It's crude; we were not raised in church. But the concept was the same!

THE DALAI LAMA & THE NORTHERN GATEWAY (TORONTO, CANADA)

Lastly, I want to add an excerpt here by Dutch Sheets, in context with this subject regarding spiritual gateways into cities, territories, regions and nations. It offers a perfect example and mirrors what happened to Paul in Philippi. And although Dutch doesn't explicitly mention apostles in this particular excerpt, it profoundly exemplifies the importance of the apostolic ministry (to rally the troops and gather the intercessors) not only as doors openers, but also as door closers—denying access to spiritual powers. As follows:

> In the early spring of 2004, we received notice of the plans of the Dalai Lama to travel to Toronto, Canada, and release 722 occult Tibetan spirits into the Great Lakes Northern Gate of our country. The Spirit of God raised up a great army to prevent this from happening. He inspired us to gather a team at Sault Ste. Marie, Canada, to equip them in the ways of territorial warfare and deliverance, and as one Body begin **the process of dismantling the defilements in this gateway.** We then bound the local demonic spirits thus negating their ability to invite the 722 demonic spirits into the spiritual landscape of this region.
>
> The result was immediate: the Dalai Lama himself said, "Toronto is a very hard place; I could not accomplish what I planned to do." In other words, **he could not release the 722 occult spirits into this very important northern gateway, and had to take them home with him.**

That is praying with authority! It pleases our Captain when we take the authority He has won back for us and enforce His victory. We should never waste what His heroic efforts achieved.

I love Christ's trophy acceptance speech in Matthew 28:16–20 (NASB), after the cross and the resurrection. The disciples had been told to go *"to the mountain which Jesus had designated"* (v.16), and there He made His great declaration of victory: *"All authority has been given to Me in heaven and on earth"* (v.18).

Again, authority is *exousia,* the same word translated domain at Christ's temptation when Satan used it regarding his authority. Jesus was proclaiming, once and for all, *"Satan doesn't have it anymore! I took it back, and I have all authority—not only in heaven, but on earth as well."* [2]

❖

CHAPTER 11

The Nations of the World

STRATEGIC GATEWAYS

B iblically speaking, gateways also represent the NATIONS, (as you read on, it will speak for itself). It should be abundantly clear by now, that gates are not just for the farm! We know that Jesus is THE GATE. So let's continue.

In the Amplified version of the bible it reveals clearly that God's love for the world is unequivocal, "For God so [greatly] loved and dearly prized the world," and this world is comprised of NATIONS.

So then the bible clearly speaks of God's love for the nations very specifically. Another example is found in the book of Psalms, where it says:

That your ways may be known on earth, your salvation **AMONG
ALL NATIONS.** May the peoples praise you, God; may all the
peoples praise you. May the NATIONS be glad and sing for joy,
for you rule the peoples with equity and guide the NATIONS of
the earth.

Psalm 67:2-4 NIV

This shows God's desire for all nations to know Him and
experience His love and salvation.

Then in the book of Revelation, God's love and care for
the nations is depicted again, in several ways. One main
example is found in chapter 22:1-2, which describes the river
of the water of life flowing from God's throne, with the tree
of life on either side. It describes that, "the leaves of the tree
were for the **healing of the nations.**"

Then the angel showed me the river of the water of life, flowing
with water clear as crystal, continuously pouring out from the
throne of God and of the Lamb. The river was flowing in the
middle of the street of the city, and on either side of the river
was the Tree of Life, with its twelve kinds of ripe fruit according
to each month of the year.

**The leaves of the Tree of Life are for the HEALING FOR
THE NATIONS.** And every curse will be broken and no longer
exist, for the throne of God and of the Lamb will be there in the
city.

His loving servants will serve him; they will always see his face,
and his name will be on their foreheads. Night will be no more.
They will never need the light of the sun or a lamp, because
the Lord God will shine on them. And they will reign as kings
forever and ever!

Revelation 22:1-5 TPT

So, this is God's will for ALL NATIONS and has been expressed as His eternal desire, through His Word.

The book of Revelations highlights God's master plan and ultimate provision concerning the restoration and healing of ALL PEOPLES — to bring redemption, justice and peace — to the entire world.

THE GREAT COMMISSION
INCLUDES EVERY NATION

So why are the NATIONS so significant to God? Clearly the Great Commission is not just about building churches but "discipling all nations." How then do we do this and is the Church succeeding in this mandate?

> He who overcomes... I will give him authority and power OVER THE NATIONS.
>
> Revelation 2:26 AMPC

Different vying forces are influencing society today, in an endless power struggle. Whether bombastic or subtle, the stimuli are real. In recent times this battle is often referred to as culture wars, which basically involves, *"conflict between distinctive groups that hold different ideals, beliefs and philosophies."*

The different realms these struggles manifest, include such areas as, the economy, entertainment and religion, which all have strong power structures that attempt to shape society according to specific agendas. Such forces compete for mastery.

That's why certain areas have dominating characteristics, such as commerce in New York City, religion in Rome and entertainment in Las Vegas, (quick example). Obviously there are more areas to societal structure than those I've just shortlisted, especially coming from a biblical perspective; let me explain:

> Worthy is the Lamb that was slain to receive **power**, and **riches**, and **wisdom**, and **strength**, and **honour**, and **glory**, and **blessing**.
>
> Revelation 5:12 KJV

When we speak of discipling the nations, we are speaking of the seven pillars or gateways of society, which correspond with the seven attributes mentioned above. According to Johnny Enlow their parallels are as following:

Power = Government
Riches = Economy
Wisdom = Education
Strength = Family
Honour = Religion
Glory = The Arts (Entertainment)
Blessing = Media

We are to conquer and disciple each area for Christ and then deliver them unto Him, "The kingdoms of this world are become the kingdoms of our Lord, and of his Christ; and he shall reign for ever and ever" (Revelation 11:15 KJV).

This concept is not new of course, in the mid-70's the founder of Youth With a Mission (YWAM), Loren Cunningham, and founder of Campus Crusade, Bill

Bright, were developing strategy surrounding **"The Seven Mountains of Societal Influence."** They felt that their God-given mandate was to bring godly change to each nation by reaching its seven mountains of influence.

They understood that the **Great Commission** was not to build churches but to build people (make disciples), in EVERY nation. It's like comparing apples and oranges, but I prefer, pillar or gateway opposed to mountain, when I'm teaching this subject but it really doesn't make much difference. It's not a case of semantics, the concept is the same.

We must recognise that this heavenly mandate already rests on every generation.

> Go then and *make disciples of all the NATIONS*, baptising them into the name of the Father and of the Son and of the Holy Spirit.
>
> Matthew 28:19 AMPC

For the Body of Christ to truly have an impact on what shapes the culture, it must first influence each of the seven major infrastructures, pillars or gateways, already mentioned: Media, Government, Education, Economy, Family, Religion and The Arts (Entertainment).

SPIRITUAL GATEWAYS

To repeat, there are gateways in societies, in cities, countries and nations. These represent places of authority. In Proverbs 31:23 for example it says that, "Her husband is **known in the gates**," of the city. In addition to that, at the end in verse 31 it says, "Let her own works praise her in the **gates**."

141

If this represents the church, it proves the point that Jesus (her husband) wants his bride the Church to have influence in the "city gates" and not to leave that up to the secular world to control such things. We must not be afraid to have influence in all these areas. This was always God's plan.

> Her husband is **known in the gates,** when he sitteth among the elders of the land... Give her of the fruit of her hands; and let her own works praise her in the gates.
>
> Proverbs 31:23, 31 NKJV

Over the years and depending on who has been teaching this subject, they have been called "mountains," "pillars," "gateways," or even "walls" (such as Jericho), in context with something that we must conquer. Regardless of names however, the revelation is the same.

INFORMATION GATEWAYS:
(ACCESS TO ULTIMATE CONTROL)

We've talked for years about the "information gateways" and that if we capture those particular gateways, then we capture the city. It's strategic. I've always taught my students, **"Faith without strategy is dead."**

This is a big issue. Just think. Those who seek ultimate control over peoples, cities, towns and nations, must do so by first controlling access to information. It's a no brainer as far as I am concerned and it's been going on for generations — yet never before as now — when the proliferation of the Internet has presented real challenges to global governments.

In China for example, they discovered that trying to control the information outflow was virtually impossible, so instead they blocked it and created their own. Which is why YouTube, Facebook, Twitter and the like, have been blocked in China and replaced with such things as: WeChat, Baidu, RenRen, Youku, Weibo and others.

THE MISSION FIELD

In this vein, we can stop viewing things in terms of secular or non-secular and see each area that we are called to as the mission field. Seeing also that kingdom strategies are already in place and that God prepares us for specific mission fields. For example each field has its adjoining spiritual warfare and we must be ready.

Those with the God-given mission to influence the economy through entrepreneurial innovation or stockbroking for example will need a specific preparation. Freedom from the spirit of mammon, greed or the love of money would have to be completely overcome on a personal level, if ever one hoped to overcome in that field. Where we are compromised, that's where we fail.

DEFEATING THE "ITES" OF YOUR PROMISED LAND:

The "ites" in our personal promised land must be beaten, to avoid defeat on the wider mission field.

> As the Eternal, your True God, is bringing you into the land where you're going to live when you cross the Jordan, He'll drive out many nations ahead of you, **Hittites, Girgashites, Amorites, Canaanites, Perizzites, Hivites,** and **Jebusites,** seven nations that are bigger and stronger than you are. **The**

Eternal your God will put them in your power. You must crush them; destroy them completely! ***Don't make any treaties with them,*** and don't show them any mercy.

Deuteronomy 7:1-2 VOICE

Each of the "-ites" mentioned above — **Hitt-ites, Girgash-ites, Amor-ites, Canaan-ites, Perizz-ites, Hiv-ites,** and **Jebus-ites,** obviously represent seven areas of spiritual warfare or oppression that we overcome as we pursue our God given mandate. This is something that I have been teaching for many years. These seven "-ites" coincide with the seven pillars or gateways that we are discussing here, (but we'll go into more detail about the "-ites" at a later point).

For now, let me say that there are *governing principalities* in each of the seven areas that will perceive us as hostiles and not as friendlies. The battle will rage and unless our motives are pure, we will be forced into quick retreat. Our only leverage is God and His *pattern.* Our success is totally reliant on our full compliance.

I seek not mine own will, but the will of the Father which hath sent me. ... I came down from heaven, not to do mine own will, but the will of him that sent me.

John 5:30; 6:38 KJVS

We are not like dangerous free radicals that disrupt the body and cause disease and dysfunction; instead we are of the breed that grasps the beneficial dynamics of divine-cooperation.

Navy Seals, once their mission objectives are set, their training and stick-to-it-ness fulfils the mission at all costs.

Our security is in our training and God's instruction. His favour and power meet us on the job, He is equal-to-and-much-more-than anything that we will ever face.

So, like Moses we must follow and obey heaven's instructions to the ninth degree, building according to heaven's pattern and not ours, "Look that thou make them after their **pattern,** which was shewed thee in the mount." "Study the **design** you were given on the mountain and make everything accordingly" (Exodus 25:40 KJVS/MSG).

DISCIPLING THE NATIONS

The word "nation" or "the nations," is mentioned hundreds of times throughout scripture (over 300 times). God simply thinks bigger than we do. Considering that the Great Commission could have said, "make disciples of all church converts, souls or even men." Instead it uses "nations." Again, why is this significant?

According to the Strong's Concordance G1484 "nations" applies: "a *race* (as of the same *habit*) that is a *tribe;* specifically a *foreign (non-Jewish)* one (usually by implication *pagan*): - Gentile, heathen, people... the human family, tribe, group." Basically referring to anyone who is not already worshipping the one true God. It's all encompassing. No one slips the radar. God is no racist.

The commission includes everyone. No one is excluded. It includes every race, every tribe, every foreigner, every pagan, every gentile and heathen (godless), everybody in the human family, every conceivable people group on earth. They all matter, no matter what their current habits or customs (current culture). Think of it.

My interpretation of "all nations" in context with the Great Commission, refers to "ALL those who are currently outside of God," regardless of who they are and where they come from.

- "The Lord is... **not willing that any should perish**" (2 Peter 3:9 KJV).

- "I give unto them eternal life; and they **shall never perish**, neither shall any man pluck them out of my hand" (John 10:28 KJV).

HIS DESIRE IS FOR THE NATIONS

OLD TESTAMENT EXAMPLES:

- "Thou shalt be a father of many **nations**..." (Genesis 17:4-6 KJV)

- "Abraham shall surely become a great and mighty **nation**, and all the **nations** of the earth shall be blessed in him" (Genesis 18:18 KJV).

- "Ask of Me, and I will give You the **nations**..."(Psalm 2:8 NKJV)

- "I have this day set thee over the **nations**..." (Jeremiah 1:10 KJV)

- "The **desire of all nations** shall come..." (Haggai 2:7 KJV)

NEW TESTAMENT EXAMPLES:

- "My house shall be called of all **nations** the house of prayer..." (Mark 11:17 KJV)

- "In thee shall all **nations** be blessed" (Galatians 3:8 KJV).

- "Who through faith subdued **kingdoms**..." (Hebrews 11:33 KJV)

- "To him will I give power over the **nations**" (Revelation 2:26 KJV).

- "That he should deceive the **nations** no more..." (Revelation 20:3 KJV)

- "For the healing of the **nations**" (Revelation 22:2 KJV).

Clearly our seven-fold mission is to disciple the "nations" using God's seven-fold strategy plan. Once captured for Jesus, these seven major culture-bending society-influencing pillars or spiritual gateways, will help us fulfil the Great Commission, given us in Matthew 28:19.

❖

CHAPTER 12

Staying under the Right Spiritual Covering

INVINCIBLE PROTECTION

To begin with, spiritual covering comes from several sources. First God, then mentorship (spiritual fathers or mothers) and then the faith community. For example the bible says not to forsake the fellowship of the brethren, because this provides a measure of covering and protection. There's safety in numbers, and being part of a global family is advantageous.

We will look at mentorship at length below, but first our spiritual covering comes directly from God, and there is none more endearing example of this than in Psalm 91, which reveals the Father heart of God, which desires to cover and protect His own.

There are many more examples of course, but we will only look at a few. Here in Matthew 23:37-38 it says, **"How often I wanted to gather your children together [around Me], as a hen gathers her chicks under her wings,** and you were unwilling... completely abandoned by God and destitute of His protection!"** (AMP) This highlights, that without willingly yielding to God's protection we are most vulnerable.

THE MENTOR-PROTÉGÉ RELATIONSHIP

This is a recurring theme in the bible and the relationship between Elijah and Elisha is a prime example, but there are others. Firstly, let me say that spiritual maturity develops over much time and God uses other people to soften our rough edges. And those in positions of spiritual authority to mould us. The discipleship program Jesus instigated — go make disciples of all nations — is still going.

There is a transfer and throughout the bible, wisdom, authority, anointing, gifts etc., have been passed on or down. Let's explore the following examples:

ELIJAH AND ELISHA:

Starting with this prime example, Elijah's mantle fell to Elisha, signifying the transfer of prophetic authority and anointing, witnessed by the sons of the prophets who said, "The spirit of Elijah rests on Elisha" (see 2 Kings 2:15).

SIDE NOTE:

Many today would want to ask, "What was Elisha supposed to be continuing?" Or, "Why didn't he have his own anointing, why did he need Elijah's?" And, "Why couldn't he be himself or be independent and do his own thing!"

The answer is found in 2 Kings chapter 2, where the transfer of Elijah's anointing to Elisha symbolises the passing of prophetic authority but also responsibility. When folks cry out for spiritual power, they don't always desire what comes with it! AND if there's anything you will discover about the anointing, it's that secular narcissism doesn't gel with it. They are 100% mutually exclusive.

This refers to two or more events or conditions that cannot occur at the same time. If one event happens, the other cannot. For example, flipping a coin results in either heads or tails, but not both. Likewise, as disciples of Christ we are called to "self demotion" not "self promotion."

This means we cannot take up our cross daily and follow Christ with a spirit of narcissism. These two things are going in opposite directions. (So if you want the anointing in your life, you must ditch one for the other. They don't coexist).

SPIRITUAL INHERITANCE:
(THE WORK MUST GO ON)

Returning to our key point; Elijah was a major prophet in Israel, and his assignment in calling the people back to God was crucial. So when he was taken up to heaven in a whirlwind, there had to be a successor who would "inherit" this role (and not someone with an independent spirit!)

The work must always go on; it can't die with the previous generation. It must go from faith to faith and glory to glory. In fact Elisha received a double portion of Elijah's spirit. Signifying how important continuity is to God's overall plan.

The Holy Spirit is a good finisher. He's faithful to complete what He starts (Philippians 1:6; 2:13; Romans 8:28). Ultimately the purpose of this "transfer" was to continue the prophetic ministry in earnest, which had begun in Elijah.

Elisha was to carry on his spiritual father/mentor's mission; confronting idolatry, guiding kings, and performing miracles, to demonstrate the power and authority of God in Israel. Crucial for maintaining Elijah's prophetic witness and spiritual leadership—especially during a challenging time for the nation. Other brief examples include:

MOSES AND JOSHUA:

Moses mentored Joshua, who was filled with the spirit of wisdom after Moses laid his hands on him, "Now Joshua the son of Nun was filled with the spirit of wisdom, for Moses had laid his hands on him; so the sons of Israel listened to him and did as the LORD commanded Moses" (Deuteronomy 34:9 AMP). Joshua went on to lead Israel into the Promised Land.

NAOMI AND RUTH:

Naomi guided her daughter-in-law Ruth with wisdom and faith, leading to Ruth's marriage to Boaz and her inclusion in the lineage of Jesus (Ruth 1-4).

PAUL AND TIMOTHY:

The apostle Paul was Timothy's spiritual mentor/father. "Timothy, you are my true spiritual son in the faith" (1 Timothy 1:2 TPT). As a result Paul imparted wisdom, encouragement, and instruction to his "son" who became a key leader in the early church.

JESUS AND HIS DISCIPLES:

Jesus mentored His disciples, equipping them with teachings, parables, and firsthand experiences of ministry. After His ascension, they carried on His work, spreading the gospel and performing miracles in His name. This relationship exemplifies how spiritual guidance and empowerment are passed down.

These examples highlight the importance of mentorship in spiritual growth and the continuity of God's work through generations. Each of these relationships demonstrates the flow of spiritual wisdom, authority, and anointing from a mentor to a protégé, ensuring the continuation of God's purpose and mission.

THE BENEFITS OF SPIRITUAL COVERING

Staying under the right spiritual covering is a concept that emphasises the protective and nurturing aspect of being under the guidance and authority of spiritual leadership. This covering offers several benefits:

PROTECTION:

Being under spiritual covering provides protection from demonic influences or spiritual attack. This is akin to being under God's wings or within His fortress, as described in Psalm 91, where those who dwell within the intimate shelter of the Most High find ongoing refuge.

GUIDANCE AND WISDOM:

Spiritual leaders offer wisdom, teaching, and correction, helping individuals navigate their spiritual journeys and avoid spiritual pitfalls.

ACCOUNTABILITY:

Being under spiritual covering also means being accountable to others. This is a big one—as mentioned numerous times in this book—accountability is everything. There are many benefits and it provides countless safeguards, especially against straying from biblical teachings or falling into error.

Let me also mention briefly the concept of the "cursed son syndrome" where vital *accountability* has been shipwrecked or hijacked. Which creates spiritual hippies, who don't want any accountability. They want to be "open" to everything (and everyone) but "believe" nothing. There is no trust.

Illegitimate spiritual sons or daughters, have orphan spirits and a wanderlust. They are ineffective and unfruitful, (this is a travesty).

The first role for any of us is servanthood. Like Jesus showed us. Christianity is laying down our lives for others and discipleship is about spiritual maturity with an emphasis on spiritual instruction and "equipping" for works of service. To get the most out of spiritual covering, we need to be *committed.* This is the prerequisite of being effective, especially in the body of Christ where the spirit of independence, is not native.

SUPPORT:

Being under spiritual covering means enjoying essential prayer support; an essential source of strength and encouragement.

GROWTH AND DISCIPLESHIP:

Spiritual covering helps individuals grow in their faith and understanding of scripture; to interpret and apply the teachings of the bible correctly and living them out faithfully (2 Timothy 2:15).

DIVINE ORDER BY THE SPIRIT:

The concept of spiritual covering is not just for the individual but also for the wider body. This aligns with the order of the Holy Spirit, where leaders are appointed to shepherd the flock, ensuring the well-being of the whole faith community.

SPIRITUAL COVERING IN THE NEW TESTAMENT:

We see examples of spiritual covering in the relationships between the apostles and the early church, where guidance, teaching, and accountability were provided for the spiritual growth and protection of believers.

Overall, staying under the right spiritual covering is seen as a way to remain within the sphere of God's protection and blessing, while actively participating in the ongoing life and global mission of the body of Christ.

SPIRITUAL IMPARTATION

The impartation that comes through spiritual covering refers to the transfer of spiritual gifts, anointing, or authority from a spiritual leader to those under their guidance. This impartation is a fundamental aspect of the mentor-protégé relationship and spiritual covering in the bible. Here's what it entails:

TRANSFER OF SPIRITUAL GIFTS:

Through the laying on of hands or through prayer, a leader may impart spiritual gifts to others by the Holy Spirit for the edification of the church.

EMPOWERMENT FOR SERVICE:

Impartation empowers individuals to carry out specific tasks or ministries. For example — again when Moses laid hands on Joshua — he was filled with the spirit of wisdom to lead the Israelites (Deuteronomy 34:9).

CONTINUITY:

Again, the continuation of God's work is crucial and "impartation" ensures the ongoing work of God through successive generations. As we have already mentioned; Elijah's mantle fell on Elisha so that his prophetic ministry would be transferred to Elisha (2 Kings 2:13-15).

SPIRITUAL AUTHORITY:

Impartation can also involve the transfer of spiritual authority. This means that the protégé is recognised and empowered to act with the same spiritual authority as their mentor, often in a specific area of ministry or service.

DEEPER RELATIONSHIP:

Through impartation, individuals may experience a deeper and more intimate relationship with God. As they receive a fresh infilling of the Holy Spirit or specific guidance in their calling.

SPIRITUAL MATURITY:

Impartation through spiritual covering is not just about transferring power or gifts; it's about nurturing and preparing individuals to walk in their God-given callings, under the guidance and protection of their spiritual leaders. This process strengthens the church and helps believers grow in their faith and spiritual maturity.

❖

CHAPTER 13

Personal Safeguards

MAINTAINING YOUR SPIRITUAL COVERING & KEEPING THE ANOINTING FLOWING

Preserving a Pure Heart, First priority is keeping one's heart full of love at all times. God cannot use a loveless heart. Bitterness springs up and opens the door for all kinds of darkness to pollute your light (James 3:16). It is the fastest way to become contaminated privately — so you become ineffective publicly.

There is plenty of opportunity to become bitter in the ministry, so we must stay moist by taking continual showers in His presence and taking time in the word (2 Corinthians 13:14; 2 Thessalonians 2:10-12).

REMAINING FAITHFUL TO THE CALL:

As Pastor Rodney Howard-Browne says in his book titled, How to Increase and Release the Anointing:

> God anoints and equips us according to the measure of His call on our lives, but we should remember that the anointing is not taught - it is caught. **The only way to get the anointing is to be where the anointing is being <u>poured out</u>. Also, doing what God has called you to do, will cause His power to flow <u>through you</u>.**

> I believe the Lord is looking for those who will be faithful to obey the call. He will test you in ministry before you see an increase... if you are faithful over little, God will make you a ruler over much...

> The story of David is a wonderful story... God had chosen David because of his faithfulness with a few sheep and the attitude of his heart.[1]

BEING GIANT SLAYERS:

David was willing to deal with lions and bears, before he was promoted to dealing with giants! Success in God's kingdom, only comes with willing obedience (Isaiah 1:19). The battles are real. Even though the cross is a "finished work," there are still battles to face. Even so, persecution has never stopped the church. In fact, we just pray longer and get stronger!

Anyhow, we too must be willing to face the lions and bears, before we ever graduate to the level of *giant slayer*. "Be alert and of sober mind. Your enemy the devil prowls around like a roaring lion looking for someone to devour" (1 Peter 5:8 NIV).

All victories are intentional not accidental. The key is living prepared and not being exploited by our own ignorance of Satan's devices and schemes, (2 Corinthians 2:11).

STAYING MISSION-CENTRIC:

This is as crucial today as it was for Paul back then; whose sense of mission made him über *effective,* (a word I use a lot in this book for good reason). We too are here to serve and please our Lord, so everything must align with that. For instance our personal ambitions and agendas must make way for Christ's assignment on our lives. AND, when the distractions come, we must stay inwardly — mission-oriented — like Paul who practically had tunnel vision when it came to obedience and he perpetually lived prepared.

KEYS TO STAYING COVERED:

A spiritual covering is something you remain under. An umbrella is only as effective as you allow it to be, in other words — staying covered — is the prerequisite.

You could say counterintuitively that when it comes to God's kingdom, instead of staying dry under covering, you stay wet! You receive a continual flow or download of revelation (rhema), impartation and anointing; the waters of baptism keep running and the rivers of living waters keep flowing.

In one scenario (umbrella) dryness is desirable. In the other, being wet is more desirable. Only as we stay covered will the anointing flow and increase. Only those who are rooted and grounded, get established and grow. The journey goes from glory to glory — not from flesh to glory.

On the other hand, some folks get so close to the spout, they don't get wet. Find where the anointing gushes freely; remain in the outflow and the overflow and never take it for granted.

SPIRITUAL FATHERS

Apostle Paul speaks about spiritual fathers in 1 Corinthians 4:15, "For even if you had ten thousand others to teach you about Christ, you have only one spiritual father. For I became your father in Christ Jesus when I preached the Good News to you" (NLT). In reality, you can't heap up spiritual fathers or mothers. Teachers yes, but not your major covering. Timothy had one Paul, not half a dozen—in various places! The key: God has you covered, you don't cover yourself.

> I'm not writing this to embarrass you or to shame you, but to correct you *as the children I love. For although you could have countless babysitters in Christ telling you what you're doing wrong, you don't have many fathers who correct you in love. But I'm a true father to you, for I became your father* when I gave you the gospel and brought you into union with Jesus, the Anointed One.
>
> So I encourage you, *my children,* to follow the example that I live before you. That's why I've sent *my dear son Timothy, whom I love.* He is faithful to the Lord YAHWEH and will remind you of how I conduct myself as one who lives in union with Jesus, the Anointed One, and of the teachings that I bring to every church everywhere.
>
> 1 Corinthians 4:14-17 TPT

Timothy knew where his covering was and carried the anointing of his spiritual father wherever he went. We access all kinds of spiritual benefits when we stay in the flow and are far less vulnerable. But too many spiritual parents will confuse you (too many voices). Your kids don't go next door to be parented, they stay under your roof.

SPIRITUAL COVERING IS GOD'S PROVISION:

Protection through covering is divine provision for your life; even your children. Demons recognise if you're covered or not. If you are covered, then you're off limits! Stay where God put you. Regularly uprooting and replanting trees (with large root systems that need to be established in one location), is counter productive. The same applies to our spiritual lives.

Knowing how to receive the anointing means you will grow in the anointing. Once you've found access to the anointing (greater than your own) this ensures you will continue to grow and not stagnate. But you must be faithful to that anointing. Stay with God's provision. Only move when God moves you.

And yes, God does indeed move people. BUT be absolutely certain that it is His direction and not your own, which you are guided by. Many people have been left high and dry, after following whims and trends that don't sustain them. They shipwreck their faith and some don't recover.

KEEP YOUR RESPECT FOR THE ANOINTING

In order to preserve the anointing on our lives we must, "give honour and respect to those who deserve it" (Romans 13:7 VOICE). God provided those who went before you and pioneered. They built the runways so that now you can take-off and land! God chose your mentor to train and equip you and to impart the anointing in you.

This was God's provision for your life and all that He wants to do through you. Your purpose is connected to your covering. Coverings are not random but deliberate. If you are being led by the Holy Spirit (Romans 8:9).

I am at that stage in my life, where my own mentor (spiritual father) including some teachers who laid a faithful and solid foundation in my life, are long dead and gone. They have graduated to glory.

Now, however, I get to be to others what they were to me. Remembering that the anointing gets stronger not weaker. It increases and doesn't fade, but only when we are faithful. The key: Elisha got a double portion. He got *MORE NOT LESS*. For doing things the right way (read 2 Kings 2:10-12).

HONOUR THE ANOINTING TO RECEIVE IT:

You don't scoff at it and get blessed by it at the same time. David had to endure much at the hand of Saul before replacing him physically on the throne (read 1 Samuel 24). He honoured the anointing (even though Saul's behaviour at that time wasn't honourable). Regardless, David recognised the value and legal authority of it and refused to violate it.

David, understood the concept of 1 Chronicles 16:22 and Psalm 105:15, which says, "Do not touch My anointed ones, and do My prophets no harm" (AMP). Just like Elisha recognised the value of what he was getting *through* Elijah, David recognised what he would get passed down to him from Saul — in the fullness of time — and he would not curse his blessing.

Like Moses who struck the rock. We cannot value or devalue something at the same time. It does not work that way. That's why both Elisha and David got their rightful portion. Having said that; it was not automatic. The anointing isn't an automatic transaction. We must be aligned with the will of God, to receive directly from Him.

Even the disciples had to follow the absolute condition and instruction of Jesus, to "stay in Jerusalem" before they could be "empowered from on high." It was all about the fulfilment of promise and prophecy. This means that if they had gone to Egypt or elsewhere, the "promise of the father" would not have applied to them individually (Acts 2:33). The things of the kingdom are based on God's absolute terms, not by our powers of negotiation.

Also, while we focus on David and Elisha, these two men were remarkably singleminded and wholehearted. A quality that is divine and a theme that threads itself throughout the entire bible. It reflects the character and nature of God. Jesus didn't get distracted or sidetracked from His mission. If he had, our hope of salvation would be lost today.

FORMULAS MATTER: (DIVINE PROMISES)

People say, *"Oh but it's not about formula."* I get that. I really do. But there's a right way and a wrong way to do everything. For example when you go to the chemist you better believe that the medicine they gave you had the correct formula!

Or when you get on an aeroplane, you better hope it's got the right formula in that jet engine, otherwise you will be strapped to a flying bomb.

So, it's rather disingenuous to say that formulas don't matter. Of course they do. From your washing powder, toothpaste and shampoo—to the food on your plate—the right "formulas" matter quite a bit and the wrong formulas can be disastrous.

In this context, God's promises are the "right formulas" for us to live our lives by and for increasing the anointing. His rules of engagement.

God doesn't demand that we crack codes or decipher algorithms. He does however, expect us to take Him at His word; holding Him to His many promises (all 8,000+), "For all the promises of God in him are yea, and in him Amen, unto the glory of God by us" (2 Corinthians 1:20 KJVS).

RELATIONSHIPS MATTER: (DIVINE CONTACTS)

It's never our obedience alone that gets us where we're going. Elisha got his double portion because he had an Elijah to take it from. **The anointing doesn't exist in a vacuum, it exists because of relationship.** Elijahs always preceded Elishas.

It's the order of the Spirit. I'm certainly grateful to God for the mentors I had in my life, who poured into me. Without them I would not have developed properly. Including many others who were part of my journey. I am grateful for what each one brought. God used them in a myriad of ways.

I honour family members too, who have supported us faithfully. Some walked away and scoffed, while others stayed and supported — even without understanding all the implications. And they have supported faithfully for decades. We are profoundly grateful.

GRATITUDE & HUMILITY:

Another step to preserving the anointing on our lives is to remember that as God uses us, it is because of His opulent grace. We didn't earn anything, regardless of personal sacrifice or hard work. When we forget this, it opens the door to a religious spirit. (Obedience without relationship Luke 15:11-32).

> Don't be deceived, my dear brothers and sisters. Every good and perfect gift is from above, coming down from the Father of the heavenly lights...
>
> James 1:16-17 NIV

When we are elevated it is only so that our lives can better reflect God's glory; to illuminate their path to Him better (Matthew 5:14; John 12:32). Staying humble is essential. But also joyful, as this is a labour of love and not resentment!

MAINTAIN A TEACHABLE HEART:

An important key to maintaining the anointing is by staying teachable. Each new season comes with new challenges and new revelation of His rhema. We don't know everything and must maintain a childlike dependence on Him. No matter how long we have been in the ministry for.

Us English folk like to say, **"Don't try and teach your grandmother to suck eggs!"** The first time you hear this odd saying, as a child, you think "Gosh does she really know how to suck eggs?" All it really means is don't try and teach your elders something that they were doing before you were born.

We can carry airs about us when we have been in the ministry for a long time. Because we think we know something. But we must not develop a pharisaical spirit. The now word of God is for today, not yesterday. Remember that. The rhema is not age-centric but faith-centric. And for whosoever will.

The things of God's kingdom are revealed to those with a childlike faith (Matthew 11:25). The flow of revelation stops when we stop yielding ourselves like children. We need the revealed rhema, the anointing will stop, when the rhema stops.

We have been trusted by God and we don't want to fail Him. Therefore we must maintain our intimacy with Him above all other things.

CONSECRATION & REPENTANCE

Always remember that the Holy Spirit pours Himself out on sacrifice, (Romans 12:1). How do we be a living sacrifice? Jesus' command was to take up our cross daily and follow Him. This is an emphasis on life not death (Romans 8:2; Luke 24:5; Matthew 22:32).

Christianity is not a death cult. It's emphasis is all about our new creation life in Christ and daily following His example. We are told to take up our crosses daily and follow none other than Jesus. With the help and guidance of His Spirit, a disciple's life is a life of self-denial and commitment.

A DEAD PERSON CAN'T FOLLOW ANYONE:

More specifically a spiritually-dead person certainly cannot follow Christ.

> You, however, are not in the realm of the flesh but are in the realm of the Spirit, if indeed the Spirit of God lives in you. And **if anyone does not have the Spirit of Christ, they do not belong to Christ.** But if Christ is in you, then even though your body is subject to death because of sin, **the Spirit gives life because of righteousness.**
>
> And if the Spirit of him who raised Jesus from the dead is living in you, **he who raised Christ from the dead will also give life to your mortal bodies because of his Spirit who lives in you.** For if you live according to the flesh, you will die; but **if by the Spirit you put to death the misdeeds of the body, you will live.** For those who are led by the Spirit of God are the children of God.
>
> Romans 8:9-11, 13-14 NIV

So the concept of being a living sacrifice, is being dead to sin and alive in Christ. We identify with His death on the cross and follow His example of obedience:

> Jesus said to all of his followers, "If you truly desire to be **my disciple,** you must **disown your life completely, embrace my 'cross' as your own, and surrender to my ways.** For if you choose self-sacrifice, giving up your lives for my glory, you

will discover true life. But if you choose to keep your lives for yourselves, you will lose what you try to keep."

Luke 9:23-24 TPT

A LIFESTYLE OF PRAYER:

Being a living sacrifice ensures that the Holy Spirit can continually pour Himself out on our sacrifice, as we maintain a personal relationship with the Godhead.

Every believer needs to develop a lifestyle of prayer. 1 Thessalonians 5:17 says, "pray without ceasing". We can live in the spirit of prayer, as we pray all the time. Our inner man (heart) can be reaching out to God constantly. Our thought lives should never wander from His presence. We have a living connection and relationship with His person, not with impersonal principles!

OUR INDIVIDUAL COVENANT WITH GOD:

We have a new covenant relationship with God through Christ. But it is a very personal thing, before it becomes a collective—corporate thing. For example, He knows each individual of a family or a church. Each of the ten virgins had their "own" lamp, oil and responsibility; even their "own" individual virginity (you can't be a virgin for someone else!) So, they were individuals *before* they were part of a group (five foolish/five wise).

Most prominently, circumcision was the cutting of covenant with an individual—not a group. God cuts covenant with our individual hearts (Romans 2:29; Colossians 2:11). Emphasis on Jesus, who was the first of many sons (Romans 8:29).

In creation, God made Adam, the first family followed later on (Genesis 2:7-8). The individual comes first. In addition the New Testament states that salvation is for the individual, as Jesus' parable expressed the concept of leaving the 99 to find the one lost sheep (Matthew 18:12-14; Luke 15:3-7) and that God has intimate knowledge of us and a deep care for every detail of our lives, such as the individual strands of hair on our heads! (Matthew 10:30)

MAINTAINING INTIMACY:

Our responsibility is to have an intimate relationship with God — then with the rest of His body — as we were baptised in to the body of Christ (see 1 Corinthians 12:13). Not many believers truly grasp this and their behaviour proves it. A spirit of independence takes over. They think somehow, that now they have the Holy Spirit, God's word and the internet, they don't need anyone else. But they are mistaken.

> *...not forsaking our meeting together [as believers for worship and instruction], as is the habit of some, but encouraging one another; and all the more [faithfully] as you see the day [of Christ's return] approaching.*
>
> Hebrews 10:23-25 AMP

Some folks never sense God's presence because they are too caught up with themselves, instead of God. Even when they fast, they assume God wants to hear more from them, when really they need to be hearing more Him. Fasting represents less of us and more of God.

A LOVE CONSCIOUSNESS:

Consecration and repentance are necessary as we must continually keep our hearts right with God. This is not a sin consciousness but a love consciousness. One who has been forgiven much, loves much (Luke 7:47).

We need a heart that loves and follows Jesus at all costs. It is the consecrated, yielded and repentant hearts that are used by God. (Pride is for the unrepentant heart, grace is for the repentant heart, James 4:6).

❖

CHAPTER 14

All in a Name

JESUS!

Calling on Jesus' name (which is backed by covenant) brings believers into covenant relationship with the entire Godhead, through which all of the promises are fulfilled in Him (2 Corinthians 1:20). The bible reveals the power of His name based on His divine authority, identity, and mission as the Son of God, Saviour, and King.

Below are several key scriptures, which collectively affirm that the name of Jesus carries divine power for: salvation, protection, healing, deliverance, prayer, and victory in the lives of all believers everywhere and the reasons why.

1. Salvation Through His Name: (Acts 4:12 AMP)

Salvation comes only through the name of Jesus. His name is a direct representation of His mission to save humanity from their sins. *"And there is salvation in no one else; for there is* **NO OTHER NAME** *under heaven that has been given among people by which we must be saved [for God has provided the world no alternative for salvation]."*

"Look! The Lamb of God who takes away the sin of the world!" (John 1:29 AMP). "He is able to save completely those who come to God through him" (Hebrews 7:25 NIV).

2. Authority in His Name: (Philippians 2:9-11 AMP)

This passage demonstrates the supreme authority and reverence due to the name of Jesus, who:

"...emptied Himself [without renouncing or diminishing His deity, but only temporarily giving up the outward expression of divine equality and His rightful dignity] by assuming the form of a bond-servant, and being made in the likeness of men [He **became completely human** but was without sin, **being fully God and fully man]**. ...He humbled Himself [still further] by becoming obedient [to the Father] to the point of death, even death on a cross.

For this reason also [because He obeyed and so completely humbled Himself], **God has highly exalted Him and BESTOWED ON HIM THE NAME which is above every name, so that at THE NAME OF JESUS every knee shall bow [in submission], of those who are in heaven and on earth and under the earth,** and that every tongue will confess and openly acknowledge that Jesus Christ is Lord (sovereign God), to the glory of God the Father."

"Everything and everyone will one day submit to this **NAME**—in the heavenly realm, in the earthly realm, and in the demonic realm. And every tongue will proclaim in every language: *'Jesus Christ is Lord YAHWEH,'* bringing glory and honour to God, his Father!" TPT

Footnote: As translated from the Aramaic. The Greek text uses the word kurios, which is not the highest name for God. Yahweh (Hebrew) or Jehovah (Latin) is the highest name. Kurios is a title also used for false gods, land owners, merchants, and nobles. The Greek language has no equal to the sacred name (the tetragrammaton—YHWH), Yahweh.

Only Hebrew and Aramaic have that equivalent. This verse makes it clear that the name given to Jesus at his exaltation was "Lord Jehovah" or "Lord Yahweh." The Hebrew name for Jesus is Yeshua (lit. "God is a Saving-Cry"), which bears and reveals the name Yahweh. Jesus carries the name and reputation of his Father, Yahweh, within him. TPT

3. Healing in His Name: (Acts 3:6; 4:30 AMP)

The apostles performed miracles through the power of Jesus' name. *"In the name (authority, power) of Jesus Christ the Nazarene – [begin now to] walk and go on walking!"*

"...extend Your hand to heal, and signs and wonders (attesting miracles) take place through the **NAME [and the authority and power]** of Your holy Servant and Son Jesus."

4. Prayer in His Name: (John 14:13-14; 16:23-24 TPT)

Jesus assures His disciples that prayers made in His name have divine power.

I tell you this timeless truth: The person who follows me in faith, believing in me, will do the same mighty miracles that I do— even greater miracles than these because I go to be with my Father! For I will do whatever you ask me to do when you **ASK ME IN MY NAME.** And that is how the Son will show what the Father is really like and bring glory to him. **Ask me anything IN MY NAME, and I will do it for you!**

John 14:13-14

For here is eternal truth: When that time comes you won't need to ask me for anything, but instead you will go directly to the Father and ask him for anything you desire and he will give it to you, **because of your relationship with me.** Until now you've not been bold enough to ask the Father for a single thing **IN MY NAME,** but now you can ask, and keep on asking him! And you can be sure that you'll receive what you ask for, and your joy will have no limits!

John 16:23-24

5. Deliverance in His Name: (Mark 16:17-18 TPT)

Jesus proclaimed that believers would exercise authority over demonic forces in His name. *"And these miracle signs will accompany those who believe: **They will drive out demons in the power of MY NAME.** They will speak in tongues. They will be supernaturally protected from snakes and from drinking anything poisonous. And they will lay hands on the sick and heal them."*

6. Eternal Life Through His Name: (John 20:31 TPT)

Faith in the name of Jesus brings eternal life. *"But all that is recorded here is so that you will fully believe that Jesus is the Anointed One, the Son of God, and that **through your faith in him you will experience eternal life by the power of HIS NAME!"***

7. Victory in His Name: (Colossians 3:17 AMP)

The name of Jesus empowers every area of a believer's life. "*Whatever you do [no matter what it is] in word or deed, DO EVERYTHING IN THE NAME OF THE LORD JESUS [and in dependence on Him], giving thanks to God the Father through Him.*"

8. Protection in His Name: (Proverbs 18:10 AMP)

While not explicitly mentioning Jesus, this Old Testament verse is often connected to the safety and refuge found in His name. "*The NAME of the LORD is a strong tower; The righteous runs to it and is safe and set on high [far above evil].*"

9. Faith Unlocks the Power of His Name: (Acts 3:16 TPT)

The power of Jesus' name is activated by faith. Any believer who invokes His divine name by faith (not magic formula), aligns with His divine authority. This brings His presence and power into any situation. "*FAITH IN JESUS' NAME has healed this man standing before you. It is the faith that comes through believing in JESUS' NAME that has made the crippled man walk right in front of your eyes!*"

10. His Name Is an Expression of His Presence: (Matthew 18:20 NKJV)

"*For where two or three are gathered together in MY NAME, I am there in the midst of them.*"

IN SUMMARY:

The power in the name of Jesus comes from His divine nature, His redemptive work, His victory over sin and death, and the authority given to Him by God. When believers call upon His name by faith, they access the fullness of His authority, presence, and power.

This is why Paul went to Macedonia—by the leading of the Holy Spirit in a dream—to introduce Europe to the power of this NAME. It was never the same again!

❖

CHAPTER 15

Exalting the Name of Jesus

GATEWAY TO GOD

Throughout this book our key scripture has been Acts chapter 16. We saw in Philippi how Paul was used by the Holy Spirit to access the threshold of Europe, by introducing the gospel (good news) to the region of Macedonia, which then spread far and wide. It was a crucial gateway. Paul advanced from there and eventually ended up in Ephesus (Asia Minor) during his third missionary journey.

We enter the story in Acts chapter 19, where Paul was already having a massive impact in the region, with the explosive spread of Christianity there. He stayed in the region for approximately 2 years.

God was doing extraordinary and unusual miracles by the hands of Paul, so that even handkerchiefs or face-towels or aprons that had touched his skin were brought to the sick, and their diseases left them and the evil spirits came out [of them]. Then some of the traveling Jewish exorcists also attempted to call the *NAME of the Lord Jesus* over those who had evil spirits, saying, *"I implore you and solemnly command you by the Jesus whom Paul preaches!"* Seven sons of one [named] Sceva, a Jewish chief priest, were doing this.

But the evil spirit retorted, "I know and recognise and acknowledge Jesus, and I know about Paul, but as for you, who are you?" Then the man, in whom was the evil spirit, leaped on them and subdued all of them and overpowered them, so that they ran out of that house [in terror, stripped] naked and wounded. This became known to all who lived in Ephesus, both Jews and Greeks. *And fear fell upon them all, and the NAME of the Lord Jesus was magnified and exalted.*

Acts 19:11-17 AMP

We know that many renounced their involvement with witchcraft, sorcery and idolatry after this incident.

Many of those who had become believers were coming, confessing and disclosing their [former sinful] practices. And many of those who had practiced magical arts collected their books and [throwing book after book on the pile] began burning them in front of everyone. They calculated their value and found it to be 50,000 pieces of silver. *So the word of the Lord [concerning eternal salvation through faith in Christ] was growing greatly and prevailing.*

Acts 19:17-20 AMP

The preaching of the word brings change to hearts and regions. Strongholds come down. Again, Paul's disruption of idolatry and greed had them shouting for two hours.

> These [craftsmen] he called together, along with the workmen of similar trades, and said, "Men, you are well aware that we make a *good living from this business.* You see and hear that not only at Ephesus, but almost all over [the province of] Asia, this Paul has persuaded [people to believe his teaching] and has misled a large number of people, claiming that gods made by [human] hands are not really gods at all.

> Not only is there danger that this trade of ours will be discredited, but also that the [magnificent] temple of the great goddess Artemis will be discredited, and that she whom all Asia and the world worship will even be dethroned and lose her glorious magnificence." *When they heard this, they were filled with rage, and they began shouting, "Great is Artemis of the Ephesians!"* Now some shouted one thing and some another, for the gathering was in *confusion* and most of the people did not know why they had come together. But when they realised that he was a Jew, a single outcry went up from the crowd as *they shouted for about two hours, "Great is Artemis of the Ephesians!"*
>
> Acts 19:25-28, 32, 34 AMP

Ultimately the chaos subsided and Paul moved on without incident but this stronghold of idolatry was greatly disrupted, which was manipulating the economy in that region (through illicit trade), just like in Philippi. The love of money is always involved in darkness. (Notice how the unregenerate hearts of men always rally around greed).

HIS NAME HAS POWER

However, this incident mostly reveals that not everyone is authorised to use the name of Jesus. The account of the sons of Sceva above who attempted to invoke the name of Jesus to cast out evil spirits, only provoked a dramatic confrontation that gave rise to a greater reverence for the name of Jesus.

God has highly exalted Jesus' name above every other name. And every knee shall bow and every tongue shall confess of those in heaven and on earth that Jesus Christ is Lord; including Satan and his demonic hosts.

KINGDOM GATES NEEDS KINGDOM KEYS

Gateways serve as boundaries and spiritual thresholds; points of transition and access (entry or exit), as we have seen throughout this book. For example Nehemiah's story of restoration included many gates, with many meanings attached. And at the gate beautiful the paralytic man was healed and so on. But Jesus Himself is our legal gateway (to the jurisdiction) of heaven; to reconciliation, salvation, regeneration, redemption, atonement, restoration, healing and deliverance; and the right to use His name (with His same power and authority) and so much more.

> Know that the LORD is God. It is he who made us, and we are his; we are his people, the sheep of his pasture. ***Enter his GATES*** with thanksgiving and his courts with praise; give thanks to him and praise his NAME.
>
> Psalm 100:3-4 NIV

> "Come here, I will show you the bride, the wife of the Lamb." And he carried me away in the Spirit to a vast and lofty mountain,

and showed me the holy (sanctified) city of Jerusalem... It had a massive and high wall, with twelve [large] GATES, and at the GATES [were stationed] twelve angels; and on the GATES the names of the twelve tribes of the sons of Israel were written.

On the east side [there were] three GATES, on the north three gates, on the south three GATES, and on the west three GATES. And the wall of the city had twelve *foundation stones,* and on them the *twelve names of the twelve apostles of the Lamb* (Christ).

See Revelation 21:9-10; 12-21 AMP

These **12 gates** never closed, representing constant access to God's presence for those redeemed. So yes, there are many references to gates in the bible. But the ultimate gateway is Christ Himself. He is our miracle and His name gives us lawful "access" to all the things of God. Hallelujah!

So, through His name we have been given incredible access. But without His name the keys of the kingdom are not ours, (which symbolise major authority and ruling power). "Keys" (plural) lawfully open many things that were formerly shut to us.

I will give you the *keys* of heaven's kingdom realm to forbid on earth that which is forbidden in heaven, and to release on earth that which is released in heaven.

Matthew 16:19 TPT

I will place upon his shoulders the *key* to the treasures of David's palace. He will open doors that no one can shut, and he will shut doors that no one can open.

Isaiah 22:22 TPT

On that Day I'll replace Shebna. I will call my servant Eliakim son of Hilkiah. I'll dress him in your robe. I'll put your belt on him. I'll give him your authority. He'll be a father-leader to Jerusalem and the government of Judah. I'll give him the key of the Davidic heritage.

He'll have the run of the place—open any door and keep it open, lock any door and keep it locked. I'll pound him like a nail into a solid wall. He'll secure the Davidic tradition. Everything will hang on him—not only the fate of Davidic descendants but also the detailed daily operations of the house, including cups and cutlery.

Isaiah 22:20-24 MSG

FOOTNOTE:

See Revelation 3:7. Eliakim (a picture of Jesus) was to have unlimited control. The doors He would open were doors of revelation, treasures, favour, and opportunity. When He would close those doors, no amount of human striving could open them (TPT).

PAUL'S OWN EXPERIENCE OF THE NAME

Also throughout this book we have discussed the role of apostles, using Paul as our primary example and our key scripture has been taken from Acts chapter 16 where Paul encountered a slave girl possessed by a spirit of divination/ python and all the implications that went along with that.

However, it would be apt to point out that although Paul is the most famous of all the apostles, he was not actually an "apostle of the Lamb," which refers to those who were direct disciples of Jesus Christ during His earthly ministry.

It was the original twelve apostles — chosen by Jesus — who had a close, personal relationship with Him and who were eyewitnesses of His life, teachings, death, and resurrection — who were called apostles of the Lamb.

So, although Paul was not included in this privileged band of merry men, he did experience Jesus face-to-face, on the road to Damascus. The very same Jesus Paul was tyrannising: "Saul, Saul, **why are you persecuting and oppressing ME? ...I AM JESUS whom you are persecuting"** (Acts 9:4-5 AMP).

This is a remarkable event on every level; for now just notice how personally Jesus took this "persecution." Why? Because we are one with Christ. We are HIS BODY!

The New Testament teaches that Jesus dwells in us by His Spirit. So, He continues to dwell in His body here on earth, through us — both collectively and individually. We literally are ONE with Christ, as 1 Corinthians 6:17 says, "the one who is united and joined to the Lord is one spirit with Him" (AMP). (See also 1 Corinthians 12:12-13; 20, 25-27; Colossians 3:3; Galatians 2:20; Romans 6:5).

In this context, when His church is persecuted — He feels it. He is the HEAD. And scientifically speaking it is common knowledge that the "head" feels the body's pain. Meaning the sensation of pain is actually processed by the head.

"DELIBERATELY CHOSEN... TO BEAR MY NAME"

For example, while we experience pain in various parts of our body, the sensation of pain is actually processed in the brain. When there's an injury or something painful happens to the body, nerves send signals to the brain, which then interprets these signals as pain. So, even though we might feel pain in our foot, it's our brains that are doing the heavy lifting. The same is true of Christ. And like Paul, we bear HIS NAME, while He bears our pain:

> Ananias answered, "Lord, I have heard from many people about this man, especially how much **suffering and evil** he has brought on Your saints (God's people) at Jerusalem; and here [in Damascus] **he has authority from the high priests** to put in chains all who call on **YOUR NAME** [confessing You as Saviour]."
>
> But the Lord said to him, "Go, for **this man is a [deliberately] chosen instrument of Mine, _TO BEAR MY NAME_** before the Gentiles and kings and the sons of Israel; for I will make clear to him how much he must **suffer and endure for _MY NAME'S SAKE_**."
>
> Acts 9:13-16 AMP

Apostles suffer more than most and they are deliberately chosen as instruments to bear the name of Jesus in a remarkable way (they are like the tip of a spear). The key is that once Paul was introduced to who Jesus really was, everything changed. Only those who can see Jesus for who He really is—by revelation knowledge—can truly bear His name, with power and authority.

This is not esoteric knowledge—deliberately cryptic and obscure—but is God's truth and must be revealed and unveiled by the Holy Spirit. It is not humanly deciphered or computed but is, "discerned only through the Spirit" (1 Corinthians 2:14 NIV).

Paul switched allegiances. He went from having natural authority given to him from the high priests, to receiving supernatural authority directly from "*THE*" High Priest of heaven!

This is what happens to us, we switch our spiritual allegiances and therefore we leave one system of laws and authority to a much higher one. In the kingdom of God there is a law, but it is "the law of the Spirit of life in Christ Jesus" (Romans 8:2 KJV). Opposed to the law of sin and death.

PAUL'S PROMOTION & DRASTIC DEMOTION

We too, originate from a whole different sphere and system now. Like Paul, we are just chosen instruments for the glory of our Saviour—with given authority—befitting our heavenly assignment.

Consider that Paul experienced a very supernatural "promotion" but only after experiencing a very natural "demotion." Meaning, once he'd been thoroughly humiliated (by falling off his high horse and face-planting in the dirt!)

In Christ's kingdom the way up is always down. The process of separation (from the nature of man without God) and promotion was an accelerated process for Paul! Separation from one kingdom's government and rule, to another. Paul responded "immediately" with his personal obedience (Acts 9:19-20).

AUTHORITY IN THE NAME OF JESUS

THE KEY POINT:

To bear the name and authority of Jesus with power, we must be separated from all else. Paul couldn't be half on that horse and half off it! This wasn't a process that could take years to perfect. Jesus wanted Paul to stop persecuting His church, effective immediately and to bear His name instead. We too are called to bear His name, with power.

❖

CHAPTER 16

Rooted & Grounded

THE IMPARTATION WILL HAPPEN

Behold, how good and how pleasant it is for brethren to dwell together in unity! It is like the precious ointment **upon the head, that ran down** upon the beard, even Aaron's beard: that went **down** to the skirts of his garments; As the dew of Hermon, and as the dew that **descended** upon the mountains of Zion: for there the LORD commanded the blessing, even life for evermore (Psalm 133:1-3 KJVS).

Notice how the anointing flows from the top down and not up. This is spiritual gravity.

When it comes to the anointing oil (instead of water) our spiritual equilibrium only comes from the HEAD down.

From Christ alone does the oil initiate. And it's only through the order of the Spirit that it continues to flow, reaching the very periphery (head — beard — edge Psalm 133:1-3). From the top to the bottom and everything in between. No part of the Body is excluded when things are done in divine order.

To be part of what God is doing, to be recipients of the flow, we must be true members of the Body. Rooted and grounded. Planted and continually being established. Spiritual window shopping doesn't get it done. We never get to negotiate the terms of God's kingdom. Only those on the inside, who are positioned to receive, (true disciples who are committed and willing), get well-oiled.

GOD WILL NOT WORK AGAINST HIMSELF

Obviously the head refers to leadership. God will not work against Himself. When He pours out his anointing it runs from leadership down not the other way around. Without exception. And once Jesus ascended on high, the Spirit was poured out on the day of Pentecost (Acts 1:8; 2:4). This power was from the top down and has never been reversed. So, as God's people, we must find where the anointing is flowing liberally. Eventually, if we stay long enough, we will get fully saturated and well-soaked. But the condition is staying.

The flow runs down and never stops, like a water fall. If you stay, you stay wet. If you move, you become dry. By implication, we are meant to live in the overflow and to receive an impartation of anointing regularly, either through a church or a ministry (Psalm 1:3).

God gave gifts to the Church so that believers would be edified and would receive the proper spiritual nutrients to thrive and mature. Living victorious lives, overcoming and walking in power. Multiplying themselves by, "making disciples of all nations, baptising them in the name of the Father and of the Son and of the Holy Spirit, and teaching them to obey everything I have commanded you" (Matthew 28:19-20; Ephesians 4:11-16).

GOD'S FORMULA NEVER FAILS

By His system of training, equipping and strengthening, His body remains healthy, while receiving the correct spiritual food to keep it nourished (1 Corinthians 3:2).

You breed what you feed. If it is spiritual maturity that you want — which is all important — then week-in-and-week-out you must stay faithful and stay the course that God has set for you. The plants in my garden would die if I repotted and replanted them every week! The same applies to us of course. For our roots to get established we must keep them buried.

Whether you attend a church faithfully in person or online, you need to keep plugged in, to keep the anointing flowing into your life and keep receiving an impartation. (Fellowship is important too; don't forget iron sharpens iron, to knock all those rough edges off. Hebrews 10:25). There's no such thing as "Independents" out there (spiritually speaking).

There is no provision made by God for any lone-wolf anointing. No spiritual islands. No spiritual hermits or recluses either. Or self-employed and disconnected members. This would deny Christ's order and dislocate His body. (There's no leg walking around out there on its own, it must remain part of the body to remain functional — opposed to being spiritually dysfunctional).

THE COST OF IMPARTATION: OBEDIENCE

We must be trustworthy to walk in power, with impartation. And God will often lead you to the right vessel from which you will receive the anointing. The right person to pour into your life. You must locate them and be loyal. The teaching and equipping you receive will help you steward the anointing accurately, and to overcome all the schemes that come against God's anointed.

SPIRITUAL MATURITY:

You need teaching and discipline to mature spiritually, so that you can help disciple others. But you need the anointing to be continually flowing to you (before it can flow from you); gradually you will be able to receive more and more of it as you prove trustworthy in carrying that anointing well. It is a great responsibility, but God yearns for you to be mature in Him.

God said seek first His kingdom and His righteousness (Matthew 6:33) and the kingdom has a culture all of its own (Romans 14:17), but it is definitely not like our modern secular Western culture. Our world offers us everything at the tip of our fingers, from food to entertainment.

It is very much a buffet culture. We have so much to choose from. Even our favourite preachers are available by podcast, YouTube, endless social media platforms, audio books etc., the list is endless and the options certainly exceed our availability. And anointed vessels of God are not more fast food options, they're not on a menu at the drive-thru so that we can eat spiritually on the run.

WHOLEHEARTEDNESS LOCATES YOU BEFORE GOD:

Quick fixes are not how you get an impartation from an anointed vessel of God's choosing. Impartation only comes through obedience. There are no short cuts for the anointing.

"You will seek me and find me when you seek me with all your heart" (Jeremiah 29:13 NIV).

Seeking can lead us in different directions for a while, but the seeking must eventually end. The idea is that we actually find what we are looking for. Of this issue Spurgeon wrote: *"Wholeheartedness is the quality required in every true seeker... We are busy about a thousand things but sluggish about our souls."* And this was from a man who lived in a time when social media and all our creature comforts did not exist in the same way they do now. However, human nature is the same.

So once you find your place... STAY. Show faithful. Stay beneath the outpouring and keep getting wet. Your man or woman of God is here, don't let them out of your sight. Elisha has found his Elijah. But never treat your anointed vessel as just another fast food option.

THE FUTURE IS OURS:

Have tremendous respect and honour God in them. The impartation is not cheap and it doesn't come easily. We must burn all our fleshly bridges and never go back. The cost to our flesh might seem high but to our spirits, it's do or die (1 Kings 19:19-21).

Locate your Elijah (even your Jonathan) and stay humble. The way up is down. More grace to the humble. Develop no airs. Stay on your face inwardly and walk closely with your God.

Our Lord was a foot-washer. Let's keep that in mind rather than big ministry. Let's serve our Elijahs well and the impartation will happen. It's an absolute.

Are you ready!

❖

Final Words

Dear reader,if this book has blessed you, let it bless others. Share it, and let the message bear fruit in someone else's life. *"What you have heard... entrust to... others" (2 Timothy 2:2).* Why not sow by gifting a copy, or even placing a bundle in the hands of your home group or church? In this way the truth multiplies and glorifies our Heavenly Father.

For more information see my books titled: **The Age of the Apostolic Apostleship** for a complete overview of this subject ISBN 978-1-909132-65-8. And: Seduction & Control Infiltrating Society and the Church, ISBN 9781909132009.

A massive Thank You

❖

Endnotes

Chapter 1 The Python Spirit

1. Possessing the Gates of the Enemy: A Training Manual for Militant Intercession. By Cindy Jacobs. Published by Chosen Books, USA. Copyright 2018, p216.

2. ibid., p230-232.

Chapter 8 Narcism

1. Taken in-part from Wikipedia - http://en.wikipedia.org/wiki/Narcissistic_personality_disorder

Chapter 9 Revival

1. Hosting the Presence. By Bill Johnson. Published by Destiny Image® Publishers, Inc., USA. Copyright 2012, p137.

Chapter 10 Spiritual Gateways

1. The Passion Translation footnote for Matthew 16:18. See R. Scott and H. G. Liddell, A Greek-English Lexicon, p206; J. H. Thayer, A Greek-English Lexicon of the New Testament, p196; and Oskar Seyffert, A Dictionary of Classical Antiquities, p202–203.

2. Excerpt from Authority in Prayer: Praying with Power and Purpose. By Dutch Sheets. Published by Bethany House Publishers, USA. Copyright 2006, 2012, 2015. Excerpt from chapter 5 The Contest.

Chapter 13 Personal Safeguards

1. How To Increase & Release The Anointing. By Rodney M. Howard-Browne. Published by RMI Publications, USA. Copyright 1995. Excerpt from chapter 4 Being Faithful to the Call of God.

Bible translations

- Scripture quotations marked AMP are taken from the Amplified® Bible, Copyright © 2015 by The Lockman Foundation. Used by permission. (www.Lockman.org)

- Scripture references marked AMPC are taken from the Amplified® Bible (AMPC), Copyright © 1954, 1958, 1962, 1964, 1965, 1987 by The Lockman Foundation. Used by permission. www.Lockman.org

- Scripture references marked KJV are taken from the King James Version of the Bible.

- Scripture references marked KJVS are taken from the Strong's Concordance with KJV. Taken from the TecartaBible App, © 2017 Tecarta, Inc. Version 7.11.5. Used by permission. All rights reserved.

- Scripture quotations marked MSG are taken from The Message. Copyright © 1993, 1994, 1995, 1996, 2000, 2001, 2002. Used by permission of NavPress Publishing Group.

- Scripture marked NASB are taken from the New American Standard Bible®, Copyright © 1960, 1962, 1963, 1968, 1971, 1972, 1973, 1975, 1977, 1995 by The Lockman Foundation. Used by permission.

- Scripture marked NCV are taken from the New Century Version®. Copyright © 2005 by Thomas Nelson. Used by permission. All rights reserved.

- Scripture references marked NIV are taken from the HOLY BIBLE, NEW INTERNATIONAL VERSION ®. NIV ®. Copyright © 1973, 1978, 1984 by the International Bible Society. Used by permission of Zondervan Publishing House. All rights reserved.

- Scripture references marked NKJV are taken from the New King James Version. Copyright © 1982 by Thomas Nelson, 1982 by Thomas Nelson, Inc. Used by permission. All rights reserved.

Endnotes

- Scripture quotations marked TLB are taken from The Living Bible. Copyright © 1971 by Tyndale House Foundation. Used by permission of Tyndale House Publishers Inc., Carol Stream, Illinois 60188. All rights reserved.

- Scripture quotations marked TPT are from The Passion Translation®. Copyright © 2017, 2018 by Passion & Fire Ministries, Inc. Used by permission. All rights reserved. ThePassionTranslation.com

- Scripture quotations marked VOICE are taken from The Voice™. Copyright © 2008 by Ecclesia Bible Society. Used by permission. All rights reserved.

- Scripture quotations marked YLT are taken from the Young's Literal Translation of the bible.

Drs Alan and Jennifer Pateman

are missionaries from the UK,
who at present reside in Tuscany, Italy,
and travel together as an apostolic team. They
are the Founders of Alan Pateman World Missions,
Connecting for Excellence International Fellowship,
LifeStyle International Christian University,
and APMI Publishing/Publications.

*(Please see our website for all profile and
international information, itinerant, conferences
and graduations, etc.)*

www.AlanPatemanWorldMissions.com

❖

To Contact the Author

Please email:

Alan Pateman World Missions

Email: apostledr@alanpatemanworldmissions.com
Web: www.AlanPatemanWorldMissions.com

*Please include your prayer requests
and comments when you write.*

❖

Other Books

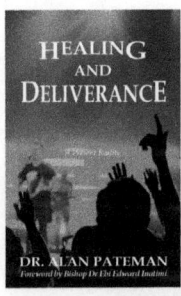

Healing and Deliverance, A Present Reality

Within the pages of this book (which has to be a "must-read" for any serious enquirer into the Healing and Deliverance Ministry), Dr Alan unfolds a different pathway, so that the heartbeat of God's message of God's total deliverance can be released into the church of Jesus Christ today.

ISBN: 978-1-909132-80-1, Pages: 188, Format: Paperback, First Print: 1994
Also available in eBook format!

Seduction & Control: Infiltrating Society & the Church

This book is a glance into the world of seduction and control, how they try to influence the Church through many powerful avenues such as the New Age, sexual education in our schools, basic entertainment; things that touch our everyday lives in order that we effectively and gradually become desensitised.

ISBN: 978-1-909132-00-9, Pages: 156, Format: Paperback, Published: 2015
Also available in eBook format!

ALAN PATEMAN WORLD MISSIONS.COM
Join us
in Supporting the
GOSPEL
and the work and ministry of
Alan & Jennifer Pateman
BECOME A PATRON
FOR JUST €12 A MONTH
THANK YOU
FOR YOUR CONTINUOUS SUPPORT, WE ARE FAMILY
Patrons Benefits:
1) Patrons monthly news letter
2) Personal mentoring with Dr. Alan through WhatsApp and Prayer
3) Free Book every year
4) Teaching Courses for personal study
5) Free Conference every year
6) Free Patrons Dinner
Tel: 0039 366 329 1315
... for those who are Hungry to be Empowered
Copyright APMI Publications

All Books Available

at

APMI PUBLICATIONS

Email: publications@alanpatemanworldmissions.com
*Also Available from Amazon.com
and other retail outlets.*

*If you purchased this book through Amazon.com
or other and enjoyed reading it, or perhaps one of
my other books, I would be grateful if you could
take a couple of minutes to write a Customer
Review, many thanks.*

BY DR. ALAN PATEMAN

By Dr. Jennifer Pateman

Available from APMI Publications, Amazon.com and Other Retail Outlets

www.ingramcontent.com/pod-product-compliance
Lightning Source LLC
Chambersburg PA
CBHW071527040426
42452CB00008B/919